THE EPIC STRAIN
IN THE ENGLISH NOVEL

THE EPIC STRAIN
IN THE ENGLISH NOVEL

E. M. W. TILLYARD
LITT.D., F.B.A.
Sometime Master of Jesus College
Cambridge

GREENWOOD PRESS, PUBLISHERS
WESTPORT, CONNECTICUT

Library of Congress Cataloging in Publication Data

Tillyard, Eustace Mandeville Wetenhall, 1889-1962.
    The epic strain in the English novel.

    Includes index.
    Reprint of the ed. published by Chatto & Windus,
London.
    1. English fiction--History and criticism.
2. Epic literature, English--History and criticism.
I. Title.
PR830.E6T5   1975   823'.03   75-17891
ISBN 0-8371-8195-X

Preface

THIS book continues my *English Epic and its Background*. There, in the last chapter, I asserted that by the nineteenth century the real course of the epic had forsaken the traditional verse form for the novel. It is natural therefore that I should complete my inquiry by writing of any English novels that fulfil the requirements of epic as I conceive them.

I have also explained why certain novels are not epic. My choice of these is not as arbitrary as it may seem. When I am aware of a serious claim that a certain novel is epic and I reject that claim I think I ought to give my reasons. Thus its author claimed that *Tom Jones* was a comic epic; Lewis Mumford has claimed complete epic success for *Moby Dick*; and the name James Joyce gave to his principal work leaves no doubt of the category to which he assigned it. I have felt obliged to write of all three works. In my *English Epic* I asserted that George Eliot in *Middlemarch* got nearer to the epic than any other of the great Victorian novelists, and some people are inclined to agree. I have changed my mind on *Middlemarch* and I ought to give my reasons. *Vanity Fair* has been judged by the epic standard of *War and Peace*; and I have thought it worth explaining why I think such a judgement unfair. However, though I may be able to give what seem to me good reasons for including certain novels that I do not think epic, I know that many readers will quarrel with my choice, thinking that various others have a better claim for inclusion. All I can plead is that I have done my best according to my own lights.

Since writing on *Nostromo* I have read Ivo Vidan's article, *One Source of Conrad's 'Nostromo'*, in the *Review of English Studies* for July 1956. The article informs us that Conrad derived most of the characters' names and various hints from G. F. Masterman's *Seven Eventful Years in Paraguay*. I was captivated by the interest of this new discovery, but I also have to admit that for all its interest the

5

discovery makes no difference to existing literary assessments of the novel. There is no need to alter what I have written.

I must acknowledge a debt to I. A. Richards. It was he who in the early twenties first put me on to *Nostromo* with the assertion that it was a greater book than *Lord Jim*. And I was glad to hear that today he does not repent of the high praise he gave to the *Old Wives' Tale* when he lectured on the novel at Cambridge.

E. M. W. T.

Contents

I

Introductory

(i)

THROUGH the title of this book I appear to have made two large assumptions: first that there is such a thing as the epic kind in literature and second that when we talk of the English novel, which certainly exists in some sort, we know what we mean. I hold the first assumption true: but I hold the second false; and I have submitted myself to it solely in the interests of the brevity that a title demands. If I had called the book by a truer title such as *An Attempt to select and comment on those Works of Prose Fiction in the English Language that approximate to the Spirit of the Epic rather than to that of another Literary Kind*, I should have pleased neither my publishers nor my public. But in the body of the book I am free to explain: and I want, as a preface to treating the works of fiction themselves, first to argue that some literary kinds, including the epic, exist; second to set forth my notion of the epic kind, defining its main features that these may serve as practical criteria for grouping certain works of fiction within it or for excluding others from it; and last to point out, and if possible help to dissipate, certain common errors about the nature of the novel.

(ii) *The Literary Kinds and Forms*

Apart from satire, which was a Roman addition, we owe our main, traditional literary kinds or *genres* or *Gattungen*, such as epic, tragedy, comedy, elegy, idyll, to the Greeks. These kinds lost part of their old character in the Middle Ages, but were revived and complicated with the Renaissance. But the Middle Ages created as well as forgot; and to them we owe some novelties such as the debate, the sonnet, and the romance. The legitimate existence of all these kinds and forms was accepted generally till recent years, when it was violently questioned.

THE EPIC STRAIN IN THE ENGLISH NOVEL

In 1901 Croce[1] called the distinction of works of literature into kinds an illusion and thought that Brunetière wasted his brain writing a book on their evolution. He was for extreme fragmentation, although for convenience you might talk of tragedies, etc., "to draw attention approximately to certain groups of works". Croce's iconoclasm never became an orthodoxy, but it may have helped to beget the boredom and distrust which people feel today towards the criticism that discusses kinds and forms. They cannot be bothered either to join Croce in asserting that the kinds do not exist or to try to order the study of them. This is a pity, for even a little thought here has its reward.[2]

Austin Warren,[3] referring to Boileau's treatment of the literary kinds in his *Art Poétique*, asks pertinently whether they are to be differentiated "by their subject matter, their structure, their verse form, their magnitude, their emotional tone, their *Weltanschauung*, or their audience". And his question illustrates nicely the confusion of current thoughts and utterances on the topic. We habitually lump together such diverse things as drama, prose fiction, the epithalamium, the pastoral, the sonnet, as literary 'forms'. All the terms are necessary, but to think of the immense category of drama along with the minute technical entity of the sonnet or the boundless options of prose fiction along with the strait limits of the epithalamium, as parallel literary 'forms' is ridiculous. Unless we can impose some simple distinctions to sort out so heterogeneous a list, we shall never escape the prevailing confusion.

The most helpful initial distinction is between outward form and inner spirit. Not that you can make a perfectly clean distinction. Take the sonnet. It is primarily a matter of verse-form; of a certain number of lines (in English nearly always pentameters) arranged in certain limited formal patterns. But attached to this primary matter is a secondary one: certain

---

[1] *Estetica*, tr. Ainslie (London 1909), pp. 361, 363.
[2] The best general treatment I know is the article by Paul van Tieghem, 'La Question des Genres Littéraires', in *Hélicon*, i (1938), p. 95 ff. Kenneth Burke in *Attitudes towards History*, i, p. 41 ff., gives his notion of the psychological and sociological bases of the literary kinds.
[3] R. Wellek and Austin Warren, *Theory of Literature* (New York 1942), p. 239.

types of feeling ("A sonnet is a moment's monument") have been thought to be congruent with this highly specialised form of verse. Thus the sonnet suggests a type of content as well as makes certain metrical demands. Take on the other hand the elegy. Here the state of things is reversed. We begin from the inner spirit: the elegy has to do with feelings appropriate to celebrating the death of a person. But, secondarily, it was thought in classical antiquity that a particular metre suited these feelings. However, these secondary matters do not invalidate the two primary grounds for classifying the sonnet and the elegy. Another possible trouble is that the distinction I am pleading for has never actually been made; traditionally there has been perfect confusion. The term *tragedy* can bear both external and internal senses, meaning at once any play of whatever quality that ends unhappily and a very few plays supposed to express worthily the tragic spirit. Similarly the term *epic* can mean at once any verse narrative with a heroic subject (however well or ill executed) and three or four of the world's narrative masterpieces. I do not see, however, why the absence of a perfect cleanness of distinction or why current equivocations need prevent us from trying to get clearer on this matter of the literary kinds.

No one is likely to object to terms denoting external qualities. Viewed externally, a sonnet is undoubtedly a certain metrical entity; and a heroic poem may pass as any poem with a heroic subject. Similarly, prose fiction is unobjectionable as a term describing a great literary area that includes the things we call the novel. (I record that I use the word *form* when I refer to this external grouping.) Coming to the question of the inner spirit I shall have to write at greater length. But it is worth doing so, for no other foundation of the literary *genres* or kinds is likely to carry conviction today. Unless they are found to correspond to some quality or posture of the human mind they will have outlived their usefulness.

Let me begin with the simpler literary kinds. These are connected with certain recurrent human acts and with the feelings it has been agreed are appropriate to them: for instance drinking, marriage, funerals. Puttenham has described some of these kinds in the twenty-third and twenty-fourth chapters of the first book of his *Arte of English Poesie*. There are, he says, certain universal occasions for joy and sorrow, and corresponding to them certain literary kinds. These are justified because of the service that the expression of joy and sorrow does to the human heart:

> Many be the joyes and consolations of the hart, but none greater than such as he may utter and discover by some convenient meanes: even as to suppresse and hide a mans mirth, and not to have therein a partaker, or at least wise a witnes, is no little griefe and infelicity.

One of the literary kinds connected with joy and rejoicing mentioned by Puttenham is the Epithalamium; and it may serve here as the type of the simpler literary kinds for whose existence I am now pleading. In spite of the divorce-statistics and the greater choosiness of young people, we still maintain the artificial fixity, within life's flux, of a wedding as an occasion of rejoicing. The few men who possess, and the more men who can afford to hire them, honour the ceremony with ritual garments elsewhere nearly extinct. We mock at clergymen who in a wedding sermon enlarge on the tribulations of the married state and we should feel there was something wrong with a fairy-tale that for the usual ending substituted something like this: "The wedding-feast was indifferently cooked; and there was a good deal of covert resentment when the festivities were prolonged for a week. The Prince and Princess lived fairly happily for the first ten years of their married life." The Epithalamium is a literary kind which, at once gay and ceremonial, reflects the type of feelings people have agreed and still agree are fitting on the occasion of a wedding.

The Dirge is another genuine, if simple, literary kind. There is a tacit human agreement that at the moment of death and a little after some sort of lamentation or regret is decent: more decent than frankness if the death is welcome, or than silence if it is genuinely regretted. And the form of the Dirge or Lamentation, which has no set metrical rules like the sonnet, fulfils the convention:

> The beauty of Israel is slain upon thy high places: how are the mighty fallen!

INTRODUCTORY

He is gone on the mountain,
He is lost to the forest,
Like a summer-dried fountain,
When our need was the sorest.

I simply cannot deny some sort of reality to the literary kinds
of the Epithalamium and the Dirge: they are grounded in
recognisable habits of the human mind.

These two kinds are simple; but the second at least will serve
to lead on to more comprehensive or more complicated ones.
Among many peoples the lament over the death of a great
man and his burial were followed by games conducted near
the tomb. The reason may have been originally religious or
superstitious. It was thought that the great man's ghost, powerful after death and able to help or to trouble the living, would
be pleased to watch from his tomb the feats of strength the
man delighted in when alive. But the games also expressed a
universal feeling about death: that the best retort to it is a
quickening of activity among the survivors. Lamentations
were habitually more than unmixed outbursts of grief; they
were often retrospective and dwelt on the past triumphs of the
dead. Such lamentation recalls and rejoices in life as well as
deplores the dead man's loss, thus hinting at a renewal of life in
the survivors:

> From the blood of the slain, from the fat of the mighty, the bow
> of Jonathan turned not back, and the sword of Saul returned not
> empty.

In such retrospect, such loss and lamentation, and such an
implied renewal of life, tragedy has at least some of its roots.
You cannot count on unlimited success, you cannot just go on
adding. Destruction must finally ensue and it is the very
condition of a new birth. About these facts the human mind
has abiding feelings, and the kind of tragedy owes some of its
existence to them.

There are permanent mental correlatives of the other great
literary kinds. Comedy, for instance, in its purer sense and
excluding farce or melodrama, has partly to do with man's
recognition that he owes something to society; with his conviction of such principles as that normal young men who
forswear female society are acting foolishly and are not likely

to keep their vows, that shrews are anti-social and ought to be disciplined, that swindlers or egoists cannot suck the blood of society for ever, that even a most superior man risks becoming an outcast if he is too proud to recognise the standard of the ordinary middling person.

But we may extend the inquiry to the less central and obvious areas: for instance, to the *picaresque*. What of the nature of the picaresque and its right to exist? Ian Watt[1] would confine its nature to that of a literary convention "for the presentation of a variety of satiric observations and comic episodes". But surely it can also go deeper than that and correspond to certain recurrent ways of feeling. One form the picaresque narrative keeps on taking has to do with the under-. dog, the little man, the fellow a bit worse off than the average, who has his adventures and troubles and somehow just survives. It is natural for us to feel for him, and this form of the picaresque represents that feeling. A second and more important form of the picaresque is the story of the resourceful rogue who prospers for a long spell and is then found out, or who finds himself out and repents. It recurs so often that it would be strange if it did not answer to some state of mind. And it answers to the human desire to escape routine and duty, crossed by the knowledge that this desire cannot ultimately be gratified and that duty wins in the long run.

Incidentally, if *picaresque* can mean more than one thing, if it serves to denominate at least two mental trends, we may suspect that the names of other literary kinds are multivocal likewise. But such multiple meanings are not my present concern. What I hope I have done is to have proved, through a few examples, that certain literary kinds firmly exist. Of these firmly existing kinds I believe the epic to be one; and I go on to inquire to what motions of the mind it corresponds.

(iii) *The Epic Spirit*

I have written at length on the spirit of the epic in my *English Epic and its Background*[2] but I propose to write on it

[1] Ian Watt, *The Rise of the Novel* (London 1957), p. 94.
[2] London 1954, pp. 4-13.

again, though more shortly, partly because it is not fair to send the reader to another book and partly because I now prefer to put the matter in a slightly different way.

What most makes the epic kind is a communal or choric quality. The epic writer must express the feelings of a large group of people living in or near his own time. True, all personal feelings take on some colour from the general temper of an age. But, granted that, there are feelings that appear to be the unique concern of the individual and feelings which he knows, consciously or not, are shared by a great body of his fellows. That sharing gives those feelings a peculiar force and flavour, and it forms the psychological ground and the justification of the epic kind. Lascelles Abercrombie used memorable words to record these notions. He pictured the epic poet as

> accepting, and with his genius transfiguring, the general circum-
> stance of his time . . . symbolizing, in some appropriate form,
> whatever sense of the significance of life he feels acting as the
> accepted unconscious metaphysic of the time.[1]

It is in this communal or choric quality that epic most differs from tragedy. Tragedy cannot lack some imprint of its age, but its nature is to be timeless. It deals with the recurrent human passions and, aiming at great simplicity, presents them in their bare elements, with not too much local circumstantiation. It teaches not what it is like to be alive at a certain time but what it is like to be a human being. But though the choric element is necessary to epic and at best adventitious in tragedy, it does not exclude from the epic the presentation of those timeless feelings which it is tragedy's privilege to isolate and clarify. It is when the tragic intensity is included in the group-consciousness of an age, when the narrowly timeless is combined with the variegatedly temporal, that the epic attains its full growth.

In order to qualify as the mouthpiece of many, the writer must cause himself to be trusted in a special and profound way. And that way will be only through a union of abundant content and masterly control.

---

[1] *The Epic* (London, not dated), p. 39.

As to content, the writer must seem to know everything before his mission to speak for a multitude can be ratified. He must also span a corresponding width of emotions, if possible one embracing the simplest sensualities at one end and a sense of the numinous at the other. But while at home in large areas of life, the epic writer must be centred in the normal; he must measure the crooked by the straight; he must exemplify the sanity that has been claimed for true genius. Only on this condition will the community trust him and allow him to speak for them.

But mere range will not suffice to create the necessary trust. The greater the range, the greater the need to control and order it. It is natural for men to require that he who speaks for them shall be much their better; there must be something heroic about him. And only when much matter is masterly controlled and ordered can the heroic impression exist. That control is a matter, partly, of the conscious will, of what Milton called 'deliberate valour', for successfully to organise a vast material calls forth the exercise of all a man's powers, and, though spontaneous genius and energy may go a certain way, only the addition of the will in the plenitude of its power can carry through so great a work. Some successful epics have had heroic subjects; and it is not surprising if their heroic impression has been attributed to such subjects. But that impression depends also, even ultimately, on the temper of treatment. A heroic theme may encourage a writer to treat it in a sustained, 'heroic' way, to exercise his will to the utmost; but this does not prevent the treatment's being the decisive element. If this is the case with heroic poetry, it follows that literature lacking a heroic subject is not debarred from making the heroic impression. Here Dante is especially apt. His subject is not at all the heroic one, though certain of his characters, Farinata and Ulysses for instance, may be of the antique heroic cast. But it is not they that make the heroic impression; it is rather the vast exercise of the will that went to the shaping of the whole poem.

If an author treats his subject 'heroically', if he can maintain the pressure of his will, he will densify his language and persuade us in so doing that his work was conceived and carried through with intense energy and application. And, in the easy and fluid medium of prose fiction, it is a lack of intensity that so often presents itself as the reason why a work, admirable in other ways, cannot be considered as an epic.

It must not be thought that every 'accepted unconscious metaphysic' can animate an epic. If, for instance, it is predominately elegiac or nostalgic, it cannot serve; epic cannot originate by the Waters of Babylon. Nietzsche believed tragedy to be possible only in an age of optimism. Epic, in similar fashion, must have faith in the system of beliefs or way of life it bears witness to. The reason for this belongs not to the choric quality in isolation but rather to the qualities that condition it. Only when people have faith in their own age can they include the maximum of life in their vision and exert their will-power to its utmost capacity.

(iv) *The Novel*

It may be that the term *novel* still serves a useful purpose in denoting a not too unorganised, fictitious, narrative in prose of at least, say, 20,000 words. You still do, in pronouncing the term, delimit a certain area of writing: you exclude the drama, the lyric, biography, history, and so on. But, even so, we habitually cram so much within the area that we are actually being quite silly when, as we usually do, we assume that the novel is a literary kind. What significant coherence, I ask, can a term have which includes within its frontiers *Tristram Shandy*, *Nightmare Abbey*, *Moby Dick*, *Green Mansions*, and the *Sign of Four*? I am reminded of the heading *Scotland* in a bookseller's catalogue I get from Edinburgh under which are listed books on crofters in the Highlands, meteorological studies of the Clyde valley, and mountaineering books on the Coolins, along with the poems of Burns, *Noctes Ambrosianae*, the *Master of Ballantrae*, and Lockhart's *Life of Scott*.

To this it might be retorted: you have admitted that the novel has a useful, if very wide significance. Why not leave it at that? The answer is that most people, including some highly reputable critics, do not leave it at that. On the contrary, they prescribe rules for the novel as if it were a closely definable affair.[1] Let me begin with a crude instance. A certain Donald Rawe, in a letter to the *Listener*, asserted: "Without doubt novels should be social documents." And he further asserted that *Ulysses* was the last good novel in this necessary sense and that the present atomic age in England ought to engender novels comparable to *Manhattan Transfer* of Dos Passos: "novels giving us complete cross-sections of society". Donald Rawe has no doubts about the existence of a literary kind called the novel and has the most decided opinions on the rules it should observe.

But there are subtler forms of the same fallacy; and the usual one is to state that this or that is the characteristic of the novel with the implication that it is also its differentia. Arnold Kettle writes: "There are in all novels which are successful works of art two elements . . . life and pattern." He does not say, "In a successful novel, as in any successful piece of literature, there are two elements . . ."; no, he lets you assume that those are the elements that make the novel what it is; and of course they are not the special possession of prose fiction. E. M. Forster writes: "In the novel we can know people perfectly, and, apart from the general pleasure of reading, we can find here a compensation for their dimness in life." He does not say that we can go to verse narrative and to drama for the same satisfaction, and he thereby allows people to conclude that the quality he mentions is the special possession of prose fiction, the thing that makes it a separate kind. Trilling says that the novel diverges from all other literary forms in that "it deals with reality and illusion in relation to questions of social class, which in relatively recent times are bound up with money". Here Trilling assumes that the novel has its proper and closely definable character.[2] Such an assumption is false and the cause of confusion. I will here pause to inquire how it ever came to be made.

To do so we must examine what happened when, in the

[1] A long and unequivocal declaration that the English novel of the early eighteenth century is indeed a new literary kind is contained in Ian Watt's *Rise of the Novel*. My comment on it is too long for my text and has been put in Appendix A.

[2] In a fine passage (p. 222) of the *Liberal Imagination* Trilling actually calls the novel a *genre*.

eighteenth century, prose fiction, which had been written for many hundreds of years before, assumed an apparently new kind of life. Each age has its peculiarities; and its interpreters, the creative writers, try to embody them in their works. Sometimes the main inherited literary modes, narrative dramatic or lyric, will serve this purpose with little alteration; sometimes they have gone stale and refuse to serve in their old state. In the latter case the age's peculiarities find their outlet by reviving a moribund mode or by fastening on some relatively minor specimen of the current literary modes, forcing new life into it and turning it into a new thing. Thus Boiardo and Ariosto, finding both the medieval allegory and the Virgilian epic unsuited to their efforts to interpret their age, fastened on the less august form of the medieval romance and raised it to a new height of importance. Their supporters proceeded to hail the romance as a new literary kind. The early eighteenth century was marked by a new spirit of tolerance, a new vitality and sense of power in the middle, mercantile, classes, and a new interest in the true workings of the human mind. To interpret such things one of the longer literary modes was necessary: the narrative or the drama. Verse narrative, in itself capable of dealing with all these things, had lost its vitality. This loss is apparent when we consider that Dryden's *Fables* and Pope's *Iliad*, both extremely popular, were not original works but translations. Comedy had already dealt with the middle classes, had shown a critical spirit of toleration, and had concerned itself with human motives. It should have been perfectly suited to interpreting the new age, but it had outlived its vitality and was useless. The creative writers proceeded to choose a minor form of literature for their purposes. This was the prose narrative, a form which, in spite of our present recognition of the greatness of Bunyan, was to the men of the early eighteenth century an inferior one. By choosing it and causing it to express the age's characteristic temper and beliefs the creative writers raised it to an unheard of height in the literary hierarchy and thereby appeared to have done something new. *Tom Jones* was the central, classic achievement in the reanimated mode. It is tolerant; it has deserted the aristocratic presuppositions of the prose romance in France, the country where this mode flourished most exuberantly; and it is honest about human motives. Further, it was more carefully and artfully plotted than the works to which it looked back: tighter and less episodic than *Don Quixote* and the picaresque romance, neater and less drawn out than the Scudéry mode of seventeenth-century France. In these two senses, therefore, the English novel of the eighteenth century, represented by *Tom Jones*, was new: it interpreted a new combination of thought and it improved an older mode of writing almost out of recognition. What wonder if, forgetting the *Odyssey* and *Troilus and Criseyde* because they were in verse, men magnified the limited innovations of eighteenth-century prose fiction into the invention of a new literary kind?

Having decided that the novel was a literary kind, men were as ready to accept candidates for entry into it as the Romans were to accept foreign gods into their pantheon. One would have thought that *Tristram Shandy* was a work apart, quite impossible to squeeze into any category. Nevertheless, into the new category of novel it went. Then followed the Novel of Terror and the mock-Gothic tales of Peacock, which found access as easy as did the now more traditional works of Jane Austen and Scott. The simple fact was that literary vitality, having left the verse narrative and the drama, broke out into a great variety of prose fiction. And, just because there existed this plausible but superficial bond of form, men ignored differences of spirit far deeper and more powerful. The process of accretion to the so-called literary kind of the novel has continued till our own day and has landed us into the muddle of which I have spoken.

It is a delusion to think of the novel as a literary kind comparable to the kinds of Epithalamium, Dirge, Tragedy, Comedy, Epic. True, it signifies something a little different from 'prose fiction', and being thus differentiated it has its legitimate use in our current vocabulary. But even granted that it signifies roughly certain more rather than less organised specimens of prose fiction it includes within its compass a regular mob of literary entities. As just explained, since the early eighteenth century prose fiction has come increasingly to express the things that used to be expressed through verse narrative, drama, or even (when we think of the *Waves*) some kinds of lyric. And it is precisely this simple fact that Donald Rawe (and his like) ignores when he says that novels should be social documents. If you take into account what the novel in fact has come to include, his statement is not far from meaning that all literature should be a social document; and I do not think he wished to go as far as that.

If you want a term akin to the novel, do not seek it in the comparative definiteness of Comedy, Tragedy, or Melodrama but in the vagueness of 'drama'. And the word 'drama' can act as a healthy corrective, for no one dreams of dictating rules for it. No one has written to the *Listener* to urge that drama ought to end unhappily or to deal only with contemporary life or only with Teutonic mythology. Everyone is aware that within drama all sorts of things can legitimately be included. And it is a similar awareness that should hold for prose fiction.

Should one then despair altogether of charting the area with which the novel has come to be concerned? Not at all. The old literary kinds (sifted and supplemented by new ones), grounded as they are on certain habits of the human mind, apply as truly to the novel as they do to the drama or verse narrative. And there is a good deal of tacit implication that such is the case. T. S. Eliot's essay on *Wilkie Collins and Dickens*, for instance, is largely on the theme of the novel as melodrama. In his book on Comedy L. J. Potts assumes that *Northanger Abbey* is just as much a comedy as the *Way of the World*. But such tacit implication, however suggestive of possible order within the great area of the novel, is not enough. The traditional literary hierarchies should be made to apply *more consciously* to the novel than has hitherto been the case. For, unless we watch ourselves, we are habitually deceived, taking for granted that a thing we call the Novel has a substantial and consistent nature and finding such conceptions as Tragedy in prose fiction, Comedy in prose fiction, or Melodrama in prose fiction, which are actually much more substantial and consistent than the Novel, remote and academic. We shall not get out of our muddle till we make the word Novel as vague as the word Drama and, when we use the words Epic, Tragedy, or Comedy, seek their exemplification as readily in prose fiction as in verse narrative or stage-play.

Such a habit of mind should help us to find our way about the bewildering mob of writings that go under the name of Novel. I will use a single example, Conrad's *Chance*, to show what I mean.

About *Chance*, Conrad wrote: "It is very difficult to put one's finger on the imponderable, but I may venture to say that it is Flora de Barral who is really responsible for this novel which relates, in fact, the story of her life." It is a remark that confirms the modern notion that an author is not always the most perceptive reader of his own work. If Conrad had difficulty in putting his finger on this imponderable, the ordinary reader has none whatever in doing so. The book is indeed the story of Flora; and further she is a classic figure, a type, like Iphigenia, of an ordinary person put in an extraordinary position. And like Iphigenia she provokes our bewildered questions. Why did chance single out Iphigenia from other normal girls to be the victim of a unique sacrifice, why did it choose to wreck the pleasant routine of Flora's childhood and subject her to the most abominable cruelties? It is possible to end this classic tale happily or unhappily; and there was more than one version of the Iphigenia myth. She can, with Lucretius, indeed die at Aulis; or, with Euripides, her guardian-goddess, Artemis, can snatch her from the priest's knife and keep her in the Land of the Taurians till Orestes finds her there. But though there can be different endings, the position itself is simple, concentrated on the heroine, tragic. The circumstances change from age to age. Mr de Barral, Flora's father, the unimaginative and simple-minded financial swindler, is a most Victorian figure; the ethics of Agamemnon, Iphigenia's father, may be typically Hellenic. But the stories are not 'about' the circumstances; they are about the heroines. The circumstances are needed to bring the old story to life, but they are not a part of the story. And the story does what all tragic stories do: it provokes meditation on man's fate as an individual. *Chance* is a tragic story that happens to have a happy ending. To such an affair in dramatic form the rather inept name of tragi-comedy has been given (inept because the feelings proper to comedy need not and usually are not provoked in tragi-comedy); and to the tragi-comic kind *Chance* most plainly belongs.

Of course, not all novels fit so clearly into a literary kind. But then that has been the case with literature before prose fiction came greatly to the fore. The claim of Statius's *Thebais* to be called epic is superficial and flimsy, but I have little notion to what title it has a true claim. And what of Gower's *Confessio Amantis* and Shakespeare's *Troilus and Cressida*? There have always been peripheral or exceptional works. But such misfits do not in the least invalidate the clear-cut categories, and I can see no objection to applying these to the mass of multifarious work that goes under the title of novel.

And the common defences of classification are as good for novels as for the drama or verse narrative. The one that I find most congenial is that a right classification puts the mind in a right direction and reduces the danger of a wrong one. If we see that *Chance* is a tragi-comedy we shall not complain that the circumstances, the trial of De Barral for instance or Captain Anthony's ship, give a poorer impression of reality than Almayer's house on the creek or the dying negroes in the *Heart of Darkness*. On the contrary, we see that these circumstances are secondary and do not require the fullest intensity of treatment. We know that the fullest intensity belongs elsewhere. Through such knowledge we are enabled to see the work of art in a truer light.

*   *   *

To sum up my conclusions thus far: I hold that certain literary kinds exist because they answer to certain clear habits and motions of the human mind. In talking of the kinds men may have been confused and inconsistent in the terms they have used; but such confusion and inconsistency do not compromise the truth of the first statement. I hold further that the epic is a true kind because it answers to positive, powerful, and heartfelt motions of the mind that can, in favourable conditions, be experienced simultaneously by a large group of people. Such communal or choric motions are usually unconscious and become explicit only when perceived and interpreted by a great artist. Though in the not quite near past such interpretations have usually been expressed in verse, there is no need that such should always be the case. Lastly I hold that the novel is not a literary kind but a vague term denoting at most a prose medium, some pretence of action, a minimum length, and a minimum of organisation. These denotations granted, the novel can answer to most of the habits of mind on which the literary kinds can be truly based. It can belong to the tragic or the satiric or the picaresque or the idyllic or the epic kind.

I therefore claim that the attempt of the chapters that follow is justified: the attempt to choose from the body of English prose fiction those works that are of or near the epic kind and to explain why it is that they have thus been chosen.

2

Defoe

(i) *Introductory*

> "*Mr Jennings, do you happen to be acquainted with* Robinson Crusoe?"
>
> *I answered that I had read* Robinson Crusoe *when I was a child.*
>
> "*Not since then?*" *inquired Betteredge.*
>
> "*Not since then.*"
>
> "*He has not read* Robinson Crusoe *since he was a child,*" *said Betteredge, speaking to himself—not to me.* "*Let's try how* Robinson Crusoe *strikes him now!*"
>
> (WILKIE COLLINS, The Moonstone)

DEFOE wrote the *Life and Strange Surprizing Adventures of Robinson Crusoe* within the quinquennium (1715-20) when Pope's *Iliad* was being published. Pope's *Iliad* is the first of the two great Augustan works that prolonged in England the tradition of the formal neo-classic epic. On the other hand, *Robinson Crusoe* (the first part)[1] heads the small list of those English novels which, owing little or nothing to that tradition, embody, to a larger or smaller degree, the qualities that mark the epic as an autonomous literary kind. Anyone with a taste for historical processes may like to put Pope's *Iliad* alongside *Robinson Crusoe* and thus create the spectacle of old age and youth, the doomed and the promising, retrospect and prospect, subsisting vigorously at the same moment.

The two works also demonstrate neatly the unhappy division that had afflicted England since the Civil War. Pope's *Iliad* spoke only for the upper part of English society, and especially for the men of high affairs in the age of Queen Anne. Writing on that translation in my *English Epic*[2] I noted how remote

---

[1] When I mention *Robinson Crusoe* in the following pages I mean the first part only. References to Oxford Edition (London 1910).

[2] p. 508.

were the shepherds in a famous passage there from the society
Pope addressed himself to. The passage describes a clear night
and the shepherds' joy at the good weather; and Pope ends
with

> The conscious Swains, rejoicing in the Sight,
> Eye the blue Vault, and bless the useful Light.

Homer's shepherd simply rejoiced, and in his gratuitous
addition of the other actions Pope removes himself from, even
patronises, his swains. They are not just fellow human beings
but useful inferiors in a society that exists for the sake of its
upper end. And I pointed in contrast to Shakespeare's "Looke,
th'unfolding Starre calles up the Shepheard" and Milton's

> The Star that bids the Shepherd fold
> Now the top of Heav'n doth hold,

where the shepherds are a part of total society as they had
ceased to be in the age of Pope. And what holds for Pope's
shepherds in particular holds in general for all classes other
than the top, and especially for the lower middle-class Nonconformity. It was to this class that Defoe belonged; and, as
Pope was powerless to span total English society from below,
so was Defoe from the other end.

Thus, so much had happened and society had so split and
complicated itself since the age of Elizabeth and the early
Stuarts that an all-embracing epic was not to be expected in
the ages of Queen Anne and George I.

In writing on the Puritans and Bunyan[1] I pointed out that
in its expanding and militant phase puritanism found no
worthy mouthpiece. Milton never wrote that Arthuriad which
might, among other things, have celebrated the completion of
the glorious religious revolution that began in the age of
Henry VIII. By the time Bunyan was mature, the movement
had failed politically and, though still alive, was oppressed.
Moreover, Bunyan's experience did not extend over much of
the social scale. Nevertheless, he spoke for many people and
in the *Holy War* produced the nearest thing to an epic of
seventeenth-century puritanism. After Bunyan (the *Holy War*

---

[1] *English Epic*, pp. 375-406.

was published in 1682), and with the revolution of 1688, puritanism began to lose its religious fanaticism. It also extended its grip on the nation's commerce, so that in 1705, through his political allegory, the *Consolidator*, Defoe was able to hint that the Dissenters, having most of the country's trade in their hands,[1] needed only to unite and agree on a common fiscal policy to be able to dictate to the government. But 'trade' was no simple matter and suited more than one kind of temperament. It could lead to thrift, sobriety, and the stable domestic life or it could lead to enterprise, travel, hard competition, and even violence. The puritanism of the early eighteenth century comprised both these sides of trade and sanctified them through a religion which, though no longer fanatical, still favoured its holders with the notion that they were the elect and blessed by peculiar interventions of Providence on their behalf.

Now though it was the Puritans, or rather we should now say the Dissenters, who were central to the habits of mind I have just described, those habits marked the whole of English society in its lower reaches; they were wide as well as strong. And as such they were capable of giving any writer who expressed them powerfully a choric quality; they were potential epic material.

How were they to be expressed powerfully? Not in the traditional epic manner, which, though it once dealt with total humanity through every social rank, did so from the aristocratic side. Homer viewed his chieftains from their own position, not from that of the private soldier, and Virgil and Tasso and Spenser followed him. It is true that Du Bartas, the French Protestant, gave his little classicising epic *Judith* (on the story of Judith and Holofernes) a middle-class setting, and that Sylvester made that setting even more homely in his translation *Bethulians Rescue*.[2] It is true too that in some details Milton repudiated martial pomp, exalted the sober Puritan virtues, and even hinted at an approval of the practical inventiveness of a Robinson Crusoe.[3] But Milton's mind is essentially

---

[1] See James Sutherland, *Defoe* (London 1937), p. 142.
[2] See my *English Epic*, pp. 356-60.
[3] *Ib.*, pp. 435-8, 446.

exalted and aristocratic. Though he cannot praise a fugitive and cloistered virtue and however ready he may be to sally forth and meet his adversary, he is not at home primarily in the market-place or work-shop. He belongs essentially to the Court, the private oratory, and the study. Nor was the prose epic of the classical Heliodoran variety more helpful. Its two chief examples, Sidney's *Arcadia* and Fénelon's *Télémaque*, were, if anything, more uncompromisingly aristocratic than their poetic kin. Nothing short of an unexploited medium had the chance of giving epic expression to the new middle-class energy and achievements.

In seeking to show that in the first part of *Robinson Crusoe* Defoe thus succeeded I do not at all imply that he knew what he was doing. If he excelled himself in this one book, it was because his subject caught him and shaped him, not because he deliberately planned a masterpiece of a certain kind. As a writer Defoe was pure opportunist, the remotest possible from the seventeenth-century writer of epic who, acutely aware of the theory of the epic and of classical precedent, solemnly attempted the patriotic task of realising the epic idea in a great, conventional, work in his native language.

When I say 'an unexploited medium' I mean of course relatively, for *Robinson Crusoe* has a kind of ancestry. Right behind it are the narratives of Bunyan: a statement reinforced by the likelihood that Defoe heard Bunyan's voice as well as read his books, for Bunyan preached at Newington Green during Defoe's schooling at the dissenting academy there and "the greater part of the boys trooped off to hear him".[1] Anyhow, Bunyan's *Mr Badman*, a life-story of a notorious man, was in a popular tradition that led to Defoe's romances generally, while the allegories of the *Pilgrim's Progress* and the *Holy War* may have been the unconscious inspiration of things in *Robinson Crusoe* that are not found in Defoe's other tales. What differentiates *Crusoe* is the impression it conveys of symbolic meaning. Crusoe is a *typical* figure as Moll Flanders and Roxana are not, and is nearer to Bunyan's Christian than to them. The island, too, is not merely realistic but symbolises a human state of isolation. It thus has a lingering kinship

[1] Sutherland, *Defoe*, p. 20.

(and probably through Bunyan[1]) with the old allegories of man as a fortress, a city, or an island. When his subject seized Defoe, he sought unconscious help not from the simple tales of adventurers and criminals but from the richer examples of the prose narrative.

How was it that Defoe was equipped to represent a powerful body of opinion? First, he combined in himself the two strains of enterprise and domestic virtue that marked the middle-class ethos of the time. There is no need to comment on his enterprise. His own varied life and the fertility of his invention in, for instance, his *Essay on Projects* are well-known, as well as sufficient, testimony. No doubt of his qualification to speak confidently of the adventurous side of trade. His belief in the creative possibilities of the middle way of life at home is less a matter of common knowledge but it is equally important. When Crusoe Senior at the beginning of *Robinson Crusoe* uses his eloquence to persuade his son of the virtues of the middle station of life, he made the tactical mistake of dwelling mainly on the ills attending the two social extremes. He was a retired merchant in the decline of life, and it is dramatically appropriate that he should argue from his own point of view instead of thinking what would appeal to a young man and of enlarging on the many outlets for action that the middle way of life afforded. Had Defoe allowed Crusoe Senior a higher intelligence and a vivider imagination, he would have alienated our sympathies too violently from his hero. As it is, we cannot really expect Robinson to be persuaded by his father's argument. But if Defoe showed dramatic tact in making Crusoe Senior employ mainly negative pleas in favour of the middle way of life, he did not himself think the life of domestic trade dull. On the contrary he thought it full of scope and stir, while his ideal of the retired tradesman as set forth in the *Complete English Tradesman* little resembles Crusoe Senior's, who liked men to go "silently and smoothly through the world, and comfortably out of it". Defoe's retired tradesman had been wise in his trading days and had thriven and grown rich. He had served a kind of apprenticeship in the world's business and

---

[1] Defoe might have read Bernard's *Isle of Man* (1626), a most popular Puritan allegory. See my *English Epic*, pp. 379-81.

had acquired a high authority. "Such a man has more opportunity for doing good than almost any other person I can name." He is a natural magistrate in his home town, he is a general peacemaker, he is a kind of economic consultant able to help merchants in their difficulties and disputes far better than lawyers, who are of little use in commerce. This is a picture that shows Defoe sharply aware of the large prospects of power open to the home merchant and of the ambition of the middle classes to have their share of influence in the destinies of their country. Brought up in Puritan sobriety, aware of the enterprise of trade, he was qualified to interpret a great body and thrust of middle-class feeling.

Whether Defoe shared the religious emotions and beliefs of his fellow Protestants has been disputed. There is a good deal of piety in his works; but was it sincere? I need not enter this dispute, for, whether he was personally sincere or no, he knew and understood the type of piety in question very thoroughly and had an imaginative sympathy with it sufficient for the purposes of his art. This is no light matter, for it especially concerns *Robinson Crusoe*, whose piety is woven into the whole texture of the book. If Defoe merely assumed piety for the sake of popularity, if it was not an organic part of himself, the quality of the whole book must suffer. But, bred as he was in the very cradle of English dissent, how could Defoe have avoided getting the gist of it into his system? His father was of the congregation of the Rev. Samuel Annesley, Vicar of St Giles's Cripplegate, who left the Anglican Church on refusing to subscribe to the Act of Uniformity in 1662, and he followed his minister into Nonconformity. Samuel Annesley died late in 1696; and in the next year Defoe celebrated his death with a poem in couplets, the 'Character of the late Dr Samuel Annesley, by way of Elegy'. There was no need for Defoe to do this; and whether or not they testify to Defoe's personal piety, his couplets are patently sincere in their tribute to the piety and the good works of the dead man. Not only was Defoe brought up under the ministry of one distinguished dissenting divine, but he attended the academy governed by another, the Rev. Charles Morton. When Robinson Crusoe keeps on noting the special interventions of Providence on his behalf, his behaviour is something with which his creator had been familiar over a long lapse of years.

To sum up and repeat: what Defoe *thought* of the Puritan religion is secondary; what matters, and what assures his artistic sincerity, is that he had it in his bones.

On the side of experience, then, Defoe was well equipped to represent a vigorous and widespread mass of opinion. And I can go on to the further matter: to what use he put this advantage in his greatest novel.

(ii) 'Robinson Crusoe'

(a) Introductory

In spite of its former great popularity, I doubt if *Robinson Crusoe*[1] was usually read aright. Robinson's lonely struggle with physical conditions on the island caught men's imaginations so powerfully that they failed to do justice to anything else and especially to the events which Defoe planned with such care in order to lead up to the culminating shipwreck. Thus the book was made simpler than it actually is, and was degraded from adult to adolescent reading. Today, superseded as the classic book for boys, it has lost its ill-grounded vogue. Of course, it has its readers, and of these a bigger proportion than for many years before may read it in the right way. Even so, it is read too little and prized too low.

To Defoe's other novels, *Moll Flanders*, *Colonel Jacque*, and *Roxana*, modern readers do better justice than did their elders, but tend to make them Defoe's norm. By so doing they fail to see that as a work of art *Robinson Crusoe* is in a different and a higher category. It is constructed with a closeness that the other novels (rightly enough in view of their nature) do not attempt, and it touches greater depths of the mind.

It is hard to believe that Defoe was anything but an opportunist in his initial motions towards a piece of writing. He wrote immensely and as occasion presented or demanded.

---

[1] I wish to record debts to: James Sutherland, *Defoe*, especially chap. XI; S. C. Sen, *Daniel De Foe, his Art and Mind* (Calcutta 1948); Edwin B. Benjamin, 'Symbolic Elements in *Robinson Crusoe*', in *Philological Quarterly*, 1951, pp. 206-11.

Excited by stories of seafarers surviving alone on uninhabited islands, he thought the theme might reach the hearts of others and that he might profit by writing it up. But his excitement went deeper than ever before or after (and probably deeper than he knew) and drove him to fasten on to his theme with unique intensity. In his other novels he could have added or removed incidents with no detriment to the whole: in *Robinson Crusoe* this is not so; even the removal of things which at first sight could be spared easily would in fact damage the total proportions. The notorious example of such a thing occurs near the end: the elaborate incident of Crusoe and his fellow-travellers from Lisbon being attacked by wolves in the Pyrenees. Now, in the middle, just before the great battle with the wolves as darkness falls Defoe lets us know through a sudden reference back to the book's beginning that he has his total impression in mind:

> The howling of wolves run much in my head; and indeed, except the noise I once heard on the shore of Africa, of which I have said something already, I never heard anything that filled me with so much horror.[1]

Crusoe heard these other dreadful animal noises when he was escaping from his Moorish captor in the boat with the shoulder-of-mutton sail. But then, as later when the wolves attacked, he was a free man, and he had a companion, the Moorish boy, Xury. Alone on the island, Robinson had no wild beasts to contend with: the arena was cleared for the struggle with himself. Freed from the island, he reverts to his old liability to the bestial foe. The Pyrenean wolves join with the African lions in framing Robinson's island-life, and they cannot be spared. They serve too to prevent Robinson's final return to the safety and the comforts of England from being too abrupt.

(b) *The Theme*

If then an episode, usually thought superfluous, turns out to be indispensable, we should be the readier to expect the closest interlocking elsewhere.

To counteract the old habit of reading *Robinson Crusoe*

[1] p. 276.

32

merely for the sake of certain happenings on the island and to show that it is a richer and closer-knit work of art than Defoe's other narratives, I shall have to describe its plotting in some detail. In so doing I shall have in mind not only this closeness of construction but the richness of reference the plot contains, the amount of tradition which, consciously or unconsciously, it embodies. I shall in fact have my eye on the epic quality of variety as well as that of control. ✳

You can describe the plot of *Robinson Crusoe* in several ways; and this possible multiplicity is one reason why the book holds us so strongly. You can begin by describing it as a version of the story of the Prodigal Son, references to which, either implied or stated, occur often in the opening pages. Robinson is the Prodigal who leaves his father's house against advice, who ruins himself not by riotous living but by a roaming disposition, who is left solitary and apparently desolate, who repents, and returns to his father (now in the form of God), and for whom God as it were kills the fatted calf, blessing him with abundance on the island and restoring him to favour and lordship. The climax of this succession comes before the dreadful sight of the footprint in the sand ruins Robinson's peace and enlarges the action's scope. It is marked by his exclamations:

> How mercifully can our great Creator treat his creatures, even in those conditions in which they seemed to be overwhelmed in destruction! How can he sweeten the bitterest providences and give us cause to praise him for dungeons and prisons! What a table was here spread for me in the wilderness, where I saw nothing at first but to perish for hunger! It would have made a stoic smile to have seen me and my little family sit down to dinner. There was my majesty, the prince and lord of the whole island; I had the lives of all my subjects at my absolute command. . . . Then to see how like a king I dined, too, all alone, attended by my servants.[1]

Or you can describe the book in terms not unlike the progression from Do-well through Do-bet to Do-best in *Piers Plowman*: the progression from the practical life to the life of contemplation in its turn fitting man for an existence where action and contemplation are combined. Crusoe, at first

---

[1] pp. 137-8.

evolution

I Sequence

making a wreck of his life, rehabilitates himself on the island, beginning with his success in making the best practical job of his condition, then brought, through his solitude and his perils, face to face with God, and finally returning to society and meeting its problems in a way he could not do in his first state.

Or, most justly of all, you can describe the book in more abstract theological terms. Crusoe is Everyman, abounding in Original Sin, falling into specific folly and crime, incriminated more and more through repeated opportunities granted him by God for amendment, yet one of the Elect whom God has mysteriously reserved to be saved through chastisement.

These accounts of the theme of *Robinson Crusoe* should have brought out what is a great source of the book's strength: its large, if unconscious, debt to an old tradition. Just as the Puritan preachers were the heirs of the medieval preachers, so Defoe inherits a didactic or allegorical scheme rooted in the Middle Ages and modified by Puritan theology. And it is through applying these inherited things to the current mode of the realistic tale of unaristocratic life that Defoe creates so adorable an impression of freshness and rejuvenation. He combines the emotional appeals both of being the good old firm and of being under entirely new management.

(c) *The Development of the Theme*

I said above that most readers of *Robinson Crusoe* were so centred in the island and what happened there that they paid little heed to the rest. I had therefore better point out what is abundantly plain to any unprejudiced reader: that Defoe both leads up to the shipwreck on the island with solemn leisure and abundant motivation and throughout the book refers back to those preliminary events with an insistence and an accuracy that show he had the whole book in solution in his head throughout composition. The opening pages, describing Robinson's "propension of nature to rove" and his father's persuasions against indulging it, ending with the prophecy that, if he does, God will not bless him and that he will "have leisure hereafter to reflect upon having neglected his counsel when there might be none to assist in my recovery", state the

34

theme. Robinson makes matters worse than they might have
been by succumbing at once to the chance of a free passage
from Hull to London and by failing to say a word to his
parents about it or to ask God's blessing. Thus it was that "in
an ill hour, on the first of September, 1651, I went aboard a
ship bound for London".

Defoe was too much of an artist and too vividly aware that
God was slow to wrath to proceed at once to retribution. On
the contrary, God both warns Crusoe and gives him repeated
chances to mend his ways before confining him to his island
prison. First, there is the storm off the Humber, in the terror
of which his conscience reproaches him for "the breach of my
duty to God and my father". But he cheers up and hardens
his conscience when the weather mends. Then comes the great
storm, the loss of the ship, and the safe landing of the crew
near Yarmouth. And Defoe makes Crusoe say:

> Had I now had the sense to have gone back to Hull, and have
> gone home, I had been happy, and my father, an emblem of our
> blessed Saviour's parable, had even killed the fatted calf for me.[1]

Further, the captain of the boat warned Robinson that he was
a predestinate Jonah and had no business to go to sea any
more after God's visible warning. Unpersuaded, Crusoe goes
to London by land. Again, God does not proceed at once to
ruin him. He is fortunate in falling in with honest acquaintance
in London and makes a successful voyage to Guinea and back,
which brings him £300. Here was another good chance of
reverting to the middle way of life at home. But Crusoe chooses
a second voyage to the Guinea coast and undergoes his first
chastisement in being captured by Moorish pirates and made
the slave of a Moor of Sali on the coast of Morocco. But it is
not an extreme chastisement. He is well treated and has company. Ultimately he escapes in a small boat with a Moorish
boy and after sampling the terrors of beasts on the African
coast is picked up by a Portuguese boat and taken to Brazil.
As in London before, so on the Portuguese boat and in Brazil
Crusoe falls in with honest acquaintance. He prospers as a
planter. And yet he fails to learn the lessons both of his

[1] p. 11.

captivity and of his subsequent prosperity in the middle way of life. He decides he must get rich quicker and, needing more labour, joins with others in an illicit voyage to capture slaves: illicit, because the slave trade was a royal monopoly. This wanton abandonment of a settled life for a forbidden venture at last provokes God's anger, and Crusoe is thrown up, after shipwreck, on the desert island. Defoe links the preliminary adventures together by making Crusoe begin his last disastrous voyage on the same day of the year as his embarkation for his first voyage at Hull.

When Crusoe, after the shipwreck and his fight with the waves, at last "clambered up the cliffs of the shore and sat me down upon the grass, free from danger, and quite out of the reach of the water", he instinctively thanked God for his extraordinary escape, showing that he was not altogether reprobate. But soon after, his fleeting and superficial gratitude gave way to a transport of despair; his regeneration will be a long process. During the night Crusoe's prospects are bettered through the ship's having been washed up near enough to the island to be accessible to a swimmer. He makes no mistake and takes every advantage of the profit offered him. After several journeys to and from the ship

> I had the biggest magazine of all kinds now that ever was laid up, I believe, for one man; but I was not satisfied still, for while the ship sat upright in that posture, I thought I ought to get everything out of her that I could.[1]

There is a beautiful irony in Crusoe's setting himself without delay to re-create in his desert that feeling for home and settlement which, as the very core of the middle way of life, he had abandoned and despised. Back from his last expedition to the ship before it broke up he writes:

> But I was gotten home to my little tent, where I lay with all my wealth about me very secure.

But not so secure really; and from acquisition Crusoe goes naturally on to make sure of what he has acquired. That done, he begins the long process of improving his lot through using

[1] p. 51.

the chances the island provides him; and with that process Defoe interweaves the other process of his spiritual rehabilitation. As Crusoe masters from the bare elements many of the attributes of civilised life, so he progresses from a bare instinct through reason to a faith in God. I doubt if Defoe consciously intended any symbolism, but unconsciously he was led to give Crusoe's culminating triumph in learning to grow corn, to make bread, and to bake pots for storing it some concurrent mental significance, to the incalculable benefit of his book. Anyhow, it was during Crusoe's highest inventive activity that through the earthquake and the fever God awakened his conscience and caused him to progress from the realm of reason to that of faith. Defoe manipulates this progress skilfully. He refers back to Crusoe's instinctive but fugitive religious feeling after being saved from the sea and he contrives that as Crusoe had several chances to lead a good life and rejected them, so he fails to act on several incipient motions of piety. And as those rejected chances led up to the shipwreck, so the neglected motions led up to the awful dream.

As Crusoe comes to possess more of his mind, so he not only masters more techniques but he ranges farther afield in his island and takes a legitimate pride in being the master of it. But he has not altogether shed his old nature, and even after his regeneration he has wild thoughts of escape. These lead him to the folly of making a huge canoe he is unable to launch and of trying to circumnavigate the island in a small one. Barely escaping with his life, he accepts his reproof. He now governs his temper better, he has learnt to make his pots more efficiently, with a wheel, and he is shown (and this is the culmination of one part of the book) as the monarch of the island with his fortress home and his two plantations.

Thus Crusoe learnt to cope with solitude and with a life now devoid of violent turns and surprises. But that is a different matter from coping with society and its ways. And to that second aptitude he must be educated. It is this further education and the use to which Crusoe puts it that is the theme of the second half of the book. Defoe passes to this second half with perfect art. He does so, well before we are sated with the development of the first theme; and, just because we are not sated, we are open to the great stroke of surprise through which he makes the transition. This is the passage that follows immediately on the above account of Crusoe's solitary and sheltered prosperity:

> It happened one day, about noon, going towards my boat, I was exceedingly surprised with the print of a man's naked foot on the shore, which was very plain to be seen in the sand.[1]

The stark and yet somehow stealthy simplicity of this reminds me of another great stroke of the imagination, in Defoe's predecessor, Bunyan. In the *Holy War*, following directly on the ecstatic account of Mansoul's felicity after Emanuel has entered and reformed it, Bunyan introduces a sinister new character, marking a major turn in the story, with no more ado than

> But there was a man in the town of Mansoul, and his name was Mr Carnal Security; this man did, after all the mercy bestowed on the Corporation, bring the town of Mansoul into great and grievous slavery and bondage.

I speak roundly of Defoe's *art*, because the single footprint is poetic not literal truth; a probable impossibility, after Aristotle's fashion. Physically it was impossible that there should be but one footprint; artistically it is perfect that the vestige of society that Crusoe first encounters after his years of solitude should be minimal: the emphasis here will be in inverse proportion to the extent of the human manifestation. Even if Defoe had substituted no more than a detached foot, left over from one of the cannibal feasts, the effect, though more gruesome, would have been less profound; the very insubstantiality of the print awakens the imagination more and the reason less than any solid physical evidence would have done. Once aroused to the exclusion of reason, the imagination takes charge and pushes the horror to the extreme.

At first Crusoe seems in his terror to lose all the benefit of his preceding discipline. But he comes to accept the consequent profound change in his condition on the island, though never at ease in mind and ever prone to invading anxieties. Another great stroke of Defoe's art is that he waits before following up

[1] p. 142.

the footstep by more substantial ingressions of men. Crusoe
resumes his work on the island; and the effect of the footstep
is allowed to soften. It is only after a lapse of two years that he
meets the remains of a cannibal feast. For two years more he
has no other aim than to live close and escape notice. Then
he grows bolder and considers action against the savages. More
years elapse during which he learns to convert his first, instinctive, bloodthirsty thoughts of vengeance to the resolution,
at once safer, more reasonable, and more pious, to leave vengeance to God and to abide the event. Having done so, he
reaches a position of comparative stability. This slow timing
is very remarkable in Defoe, who elsewhere tends to crowd
his events thick, and it adds incalculably to the dignity of
what happens on the island. It is as if the mood of reflection
the island has come to signify is so profound that it must not be
disturbed and abandoned too quickly. It must be partially
prolonged into the period after the active life has begun. And
there is great beauty in Crusoe's attaining this comparative
stability of mind; for it recalls his previous more thorough but
actually more precarious stability and at the same time, being
comparative only, foretells future change.

That change occurs when the savages land, against custom,
on Crusoe's side of the island, and when, soon after and
against the reader's expectation, a new human element is
introduced, the wreck off the island of a European ship.
Nothing could be better than this ship's introduction just as
our expectations are thoroughly concentrated on the savages.
And nothing is more powerfully conceived in the whole book
than Crusoe's yearning for human society, roused by the sight
of the wreck:

"Oh that it had been but one!" I believe I repeated the words,
"Oh that it had been but one!" a thousand times; and the desires
were so moved by it, that when I spoke the words my hands
would clinch together, and my fingers press the palms of my
hands, that if I had had any soft thing in my hand, it would have
crushed it involuntarily; and my teeth in my head would strike
together and set against one another so strong that for some time
I could not part them again.[1]

[1] pp. 173-4.

And the incident is followed by the double irony of his finding the 'one' in the form of the dead boy washed up from the wreck, and then, later, when he has given up hope and in the form he least expected, the second 'one' in the living man, Friday. There was no sin in Crusoe's longing for a companion any more than there was in Milton's Adam when he felt there was something lacking in Paradise and God put things right by creating Eve. On the contrary, it was now proper that Crusoe should be no longer content with the easiness of his confined life. All the same he was wrong still to toy with desperate plans of escape, yielding once more to his old sin of not being satisfied with the station God had set him in and of embarking on ill-considered ventures. He spent two years in this state, when God intervened to help him. There is nothing finer in the book than the account of Crusoe, in good health, unable for no apparent reason to sleep, his mind and memory working with uncommon speed and clarity, reviewing all his past life, marvelling at his blessed and providential security during the years before he saw the footprint and truly grateful to God for it, but finally worked up into a feverish desire to venture to sea on the slender hope of a rescue. Worn out he fell asleep and had a dream, prophetic of later happening, of saving a captive savage and of finding in him a companion and pilot in escape. To this dream's direction he then turned his thoughts; but God, slow to show his utmost favour as he had been slow to wrath, keeps Crusoe waiting a year and a half before the prophecy is fulfilled and Friday becomes his slave.

Blessed by Friday's society, Crusoe acts virtuously in teaching him the rudiments of Christianity and in so doing consolidates his own faith. He has now served his penance and experiences real felicity. But things do not quite follow the indications of the dream. Crusoe had planned to go with Friday to join the Spaniards who, Friday told him, were living with his own people; but a new landing of cannibals interrupts the plan and leads to the rescue of Friday's father and a Spaniard. There are now four on the island, and it is not for nothing that Defoe reiterates the theme of kingship:

> My island was now peopled, and I thought myself very rich in subjects; and it was a merry reflection, which I frequently made,

how like a king I looked. First of all, the whole country was my own mere property, so that I had an undoubted right of dominion. Secondly, my people were perfectly subjected. I was absolute lord and lawgiver; they all owed their lives to me, and were ready to lay down their lives, if there had been occasion of it, for me. It was remarkable, too, we had but three subjects, and they were of three different religions. My man Friday was a Protestant, his father was a Pagan and a cannibal, and the Spaniard was a Papist. However, I allowed liberty of conscience throughout my dominions.[1]

This is, of course, 'a merry reflection'; and aptly so, because we are beginning to get back to the world of men. But it is more: it marks a point in Crusoe's mental growth. He has reached a higher stature than when he was a king among his animal dependents, about to be thrown into confusion by the sight of the footprint. Nor should we overlook the mention of property. According to the kind of Protestantism with which Defoe was familiar, it was right that a good state of mind should receive a material reward.

Hereafter the action moves quicker. Crusoe acts wisely and humanely when the ship arrives and the mutineers land. His pretence of his being His Excellency the Governor with a bodyguard of fifty men both serves the plot and intensifies the idea of kingship. It has a tinge of comedy like the passage just quoted and yet it connotes a still greater mental stature in Crusoe. Having defeated the plans of the mutineers, he obtains a passage for himself and Friday on the ship and provides for the settlement of the island. When he returns to Europe he acts justly to the Portuguese captain and the English widow who had helped him, and disposes wisely of the wealth God had blessed him with. He ends having learnt his lesson and at peace with the middle way of life. _? Returns to Island_

(d) Suggestiveness

I do not assert that the fullness and good order of the plot of *Robinson Crusoe* imply a great deal by themselves. It is when we add them to the other literary qualities Defoe commanded that we can estimate their full weight. They imply an intensity

[1] p. 227.

in the way he apprehended his story, a steady seriousness, unique in his novels.

Defoe may, as I have pleaded, conduct his story with great art. But it is, for all that, a simple story with few characters and no very great diversity of events. Only through making these simplicities pregnant could he achieve the richness of content necessary for the epic effect. And that was precisely what he was able to do. None of the characters strikes our imagination powerfully except Crusoe himself; and he is so limited (you have only to think of Hamlet to admit this) that you wonder why he so impresses. But impress he does; and in two quite different ways. James Sutherland was right in saying that Crusoe "is first of all an Englishman of the lower middle classes making the best of things"; and Coleridge[1] was also right in saying that Defoe's excellence was "to make me forget my specific class, character and circumstances and to raise me, while I read him, into the universal man". And the reader feels like that because Crusoe himself becomes universal man. Further, even in his first, narrower, capacity Crusoe embraces both the elements, the adventurous and the domestic, of contemporary puritanism. At the beginning he is dominated by the first, but this does not mean that the second is not there underneath. On the contrary, the moment unmitigated adventure has reached its logical, disastrous, end, all Crusoe's energy is turned to making a home for himself, and out of seemingly intractable materials. Defoe stages his union of the two elements with consummate skill. He could, of course, have embodied them in two characters, one bred to seafaring adventure, the other to trade at home, and allowed them to live the lives to which their breeding pointed. Instead, he uses a single character and makes him interesting through his contrariness and pugnacity. Crusoe chooses adventure and chance when it was easy for him to be mercantile and domestic; he fights for domestic security when it was easier for him to fall into a despairing inertia and to accept whatever chance or adventure put in his way. He thus satisfies the two human instincts of being for and against the government. More narrowly he disinfects of their deadliness the deadly virtues of industry,

[1] *Literary Remains* (London 1836), i, p. 189.

thrift, sobriety, and punctuality. Over and above all this, Crusoe in the great crises ceases to embody the great qualities of contemporary puritanism and becomes the type of man himself in his struggle with circumstance. No character in eighteenth-century fiction embraces so much as Robinson Crusoe.

This richness of the protagonist's character is matched constantly by the rich suggestiveness of the incidents. All recognise Defoe's special gift of making the reader believe, through the utter confidence with which he goes into details, in the facts he presents. Most writers are content that the reader should suspend willingly his disbelief; Defoe is different in sometimes compelling the reader a little in the direction of positive belief in the happening. Defoe's method in itself is no better than the usual one; indeed it would stale quickly if widely affected. But it suited Defoe and gave him his special flavour. Now, in *Robinson Crusoe*, as nowhere else, Defoe used his special kind of verisimilitude to achieve a rare emotional intensity. His epitaph on his comrades who perished in the shipwreck from which only he was saved is:

> I never saw them afterwards, or any sign of them, except three of their hats, one cap, and two shoes that were not fellows.[1]

It is, of course, the last detail that compels Defoe's peculiar kind of credibility. But it does more. It brings home the commonplace of the insensitiveness and disorderliness of mere nature (the sea couldn't even bother to wash up a *pair* of shoes); and it renders that heightened state of the human mind, when it not only experiences momentous feelings or makes wide general decisions but simultaneously notices the most trivial details. And, in so rendering, it stirs the mind of the reader to a state of uncommon receptiveness.

Defoe's observation of the two shoes' disparity is one of many such in *Robinson Crusoe*, and these, as well as having their immediate emotional effect, combine in making us see events through the eyes of the narrator. We tell ourselves not merely that these happenings are singularly lifelike but that Crusoe was an exceptionally observant man; so much so that we

[1] p. 43.

ourselves willingly to see things through his eyes.

ords, we have the least possible sense of the author's

___ ___ ___ d personal opinions, and a correspondingly strong
dramatic sense of events happening to the narrator or seen
through his eyes.

This general remark on *Robinson Crusoe* was provoked by
a sentence that commemorated pitifully Crusoe's lost com-
panions. Take now a passage in a different mood to illustrate
the richness of art still further. It describes Crusoe's return to
the island after his second expedition to the wreck:

> I was under some apprehensions during my absence from the
> land, that at least my provisions might be devoured on shore;
> but when I came back, I found no sign of any visitor, only there
> sat a creature like a wild cat upon one of the chests, which, when
> I came towards it, ran away a little distance, and then stood still.
> She sat very composed and unconcerned, and looked full in my
> face, as if she had a mind to be acquainted with me. I presented
> my gun at her; but as she did not understand it, she was perfectly
> unconcerned at it, nor did she offer to stir away; upon which I
> tossed her a bit of biscuit, though, by the way, I was not very
> free of it, for my store was not great. However, I spared her a
> bit, I say, and she went to it, smelled of it, and ate it, and looked
> (as pleased) for more; but I thanked her, and could spare no
> more, so she marched off.[1]

Such a passage is profoundly puzzling. How, one asks, did
Defoe reach such perfection of description? how did he crowd
much into a minute space through so simple and direct means?
Did he picture the incident with so precise a vision that he
wrote his words without a pause? or did he study his effects,
for 'effects' there are? For instance, he gives the effect of
anxiety by using the word *devoured* and not *eaten*: the loss of his
stores would be a disaster, to which the stronger word is
appropriate. Again, *tossing* denotes a more leisurely action
than throwing and corresponds to Crusoe's mood of idleness
and amusement. No poet has made sound echo sense in a more
masterly way than Defoe when he wrote "ran away a little
distance, and then stood still". And near the end *smelled of it*,
with its suggestion of a slower caution, fits the nature of cat

[1] pp. 50-1.

better than the more abrupt *smelt it* would have done. And, in general, who has conveyed the essentials of cat-behaviour in so short a space: with such economy of means and with so much implied? He does not tell us, for instance, that the cat held her tail erect when she left, but the abrupt stiff rhythm of the last words forces that picture on us. The whole little account takes us by surprise; we feel, as we read it, like a very small boy who has lighted on a newly minted half-crown. But, for all the surprise, it has its own organic justification. The cat, though technically wild, behaves like a tame one—had Crusoe spared more biscuit he might have kept her—so that she reinforces the domestic theme which Defoe introduces as soon as the opposite theme has reached its logical end in disaster. The passage also makes credible or softens the absence of wild beasts on the island. Some wild life there must be, or we should be incredulous; but violent and dangerous beasts, such as Crusoe encountered before on the African coast and after in the Pyrenees, were out of place. Such skill in both setting off the passage by surprise and bringing it in so pat to forward the action or make credible the situation is as puzzling as the nature of the passage itself. This has the air of pondered and deliberate art; and yet such art is the last thing we expect of Defoe. However, the puzzlement is secondary. What matters is that the passage illustrates both the richness of content and the constructional skill that Defoe commanded in *Robinson Crusoe*.

(e) *Allegory*

As soon as we assert (or admit) that Crusoe is something more than the chief figure in a lively narrative, being the type both of the merchant adventurer of his own day and of mankind itself in certain difficulties, we have to decide whether to push such multiple significances farther. Present fashion tempts us to push them much farther, and my own temperament may be too ready to acquiesce in it. Making what allowance I can for these two factors, I cannot escape the conclusion that *Robinson Crusoe* is nearer to the sort of thing you get in Bunyan before and Kafka after than are any other of the chief novels of the eighteenth century. Tom Jones is a satisfactory comic hero, but in no way mankind; Mrs Shandy cannot be bettered as a recognisable female character in a book of a certain kind, but has not begun to be Mother Eve simultaneously; and (extend the eighteenth-century mode into the next age) Jane Austen's young women have no other dimension than that of the dramatic fiction in which they exist. Crusoe is nearer to Milton's Adam and to Bunyan's Christian than to any of these. Nor is it surprising in view of Defoe's familiarity with the works of his Puritan predecessors. We can therefore expect some kind of multiple meaning not only in the protagonist but in some of the events of *Robinson Crusoe.*

The question is: in which? Edwin Benjamin goes so far as to see symbolic meanings in the two sides of the island and in the shoots of green barley that spring from the fortuitously scattered grain. The lush side of the island with its grapes, its turtles, and its steamier climate is said to stand for the luxurious temperament. Crusoe rightly decides to remain on the less lush and austerer side, which has its corresponding moral significance. The shoots of barley are also the shoots of grace newly sprung in Crusoe's heart. I do not believe in such precise and detailed symbolism, which could hardly exist without the author's conscious intention. On the other hand I agree (as I conveyed in describing the plot) with Benjamin's more general theory of a connection between Crusoe's victory over nature and his victory over himself. Because he progressively mastered himself he had the strength to master nature; and some of his physical victories are at the same time symbols of mental triumph. But, again, which? There is enormous force in Defoe's account of Crusoe making his pots. Should we see here the biblical allegory of God the potter and man the pot? is Crusoe's success in making the pot his own success, through God's help, in re-making himself? Again, I am reluctant to admit anything so worked out, so precise. And if Crusoe's potting is anywhere symbolic it is later, when, just after saying that his thoughts were "very much composed as to my condition and fully comforted in resigning myself to the dispositions of Providence", he says that he arrived at unexpected perfection in his earthenware, having learnt to use a wheel.[1] There may well be some correspondence here

[1] p. 133.

46

between the good order of Crusoe's thoughts and the regular motion of the potter's wheel. But as for the first, difficult, triumph in pot-making, it should not be separated from the larger process of making and storing bread. Of that process it is the most difficult and perhaps the culminating part, but it is subordinate to the whole. On the other hand I cannot confine the meaning of the total process of making and storing bread to the mere acts that are necessary to it. Bread is here the token of the civilised life and of the pure essentials not the trimmings of that life; and when Crusoe has learnt to grow the grain, to make the bread, and to store it he has made good as he could not have done through any other act.

This symbolic act of making bread unites with other things in the book to take the action out of its own day and to extend it back in time. On firing his first shot on the island, Crusoe's thoughts fly backward, for he comments: "I believe it was the first gun that had been fired there since the creation of the world." That is a homely way of putting it, and yet the sentiment is the romantically imaginative one of Tennyson's

> wind, that shrills
> All night in a waste land, where no one comes
> Or hath come, since the making of the world.

It is because Defoe commands this kind of imagination that his Crusoe represents both the middle-class pioneer of his own day and earlier man painfully inventing the arts of civilisation.

All in all, the precise limits of Defoe's symbolism do not matter much, if some sense of proportion is preserved. What does matter to the highest degree is that Defoe creates in a careful and unprejudiced reader that sharpened state of mind that knows it must be ready for the unusual and the richly significant.

* * *

What I have written so far has been meant to demonstrate among other things that the literary kind to which Defoe tends is the epic rather than tragedy, comedy, melodrama, satire, and so forth. He voices the 'accepted unconscious metaphysic' of a large group of men and he qualifies as their spokesman by revealing a much more capacious mind than they themselves possess. But tending and arriving are different: and in the end I have to face the matter of Defoe's general quality of writing, for on that quality will depend his position on the road between setting forth and arriving.

It must be admitted first that the quality of style in *Robinson Crusoe* is not constant. Here, for instance, is a very poor piece of writing:

> While we were in this condition, the men yet labouring at the oar to bring the boat near the shore, we could see when, our boat mounting the waves, we were able to see the shore, a great many people running along the shore to assist us when we should come near. But we made but slow way towards the shore, nor were able to reach the shore till, being past the lighthouse at Winterton, the shore falls off to the westward towards Cromer, and so the land broke off a little the violence of the wind. Here we got in, and, though not without much difficulty, got all safe on shore.[1]

Here the repetitions of the word *shore* could have been avoided with a little care and are very ugly. But such lapses are rare; and in general Defoe slides easily back and forth from full and expressive simplicity to high eloquence or great intensity. It has been difficult for readers to do justice to the eloquence of Defoe's moralisings through being suspicious of Defoe's sincerity. Granting him imaginative sincerity, which is alone to the point, we should overcome that difficulty and recognise the genuine power of passages like the following:

> How strange a chequer-work of Providence is the life of man! and by what secret differing springs are the affections hurried about as differing circumstance permit! To-day we love what to-morrow we hate; to-day we seek what to-morrow we shun; to-day we desire what to-morrow we fear, nay, even tremble at the apprehensions of. This was exemplified in me, at this time, in the most lively manner imaginable; for I, whose only affliction was that I seemed banished from human society, that I was alone, circumscribed by the boundless ocean, cut off from mankind, and condemned to what I called silent life; that I was as one who Heaven thought not worthy to be numbered among the living, or to appear among the rest of his creatures; that to have seen one

[1] pp. 10-11.

of my own species would have seemed to me a raising me from death to life, and the greatest blessing that Heaven itself, next to the supreme blessing of salvation, could bestow; I say, that I should now tremble at the very apprehensions of seeing a man, and was ready to sink into the ground at but the shadow or silent appearance of a man's having set his foot in the island.[1]

This is a kind of sustained eloquence that issues with perfect propriety from Defoe's norm, while being very different from it. For emotional intensity Crusoe's recollection of his uncontrolled passions in his early days on the island are a sufficient illustration:

Before, as I walked about, either on my hunting, or for viewing the country, the anguish of my Soul at my condition would break out upon me on a sudden, and my very heart would die within me, to think of the woods, the mountains, the deserts I was in, and how I was a prisoner, locked up with the eternal bars and bolts of the ocean, in an uninhabited wilderness, without redemption. In the midst of the greatest composures of my mind, this would break out upon me like a storm and make me wring my hands and weep like a child. Sometimes it would take me in the middle of my work and I would immediately sit down and sigh and look upon the ground for an hour or two together; and this was still worse to me, for if I could burst out into tears or vent myself by words, it would go off, and the grief, having exhausted itself, would abate.[2]

Defoe's qualities of writing are, indeed, great; but we must recognise his limitations. I first mentioned Pope along with Defoe, because Pope's *Iliad* and *Robinson Crusoe* belong to the same years; and I remarked how different were the two societies that the two authors span. It comes as a shock to reflect that Pope was the younger man by a whole generation, so that it is hardly fair to use one of the two to illustrate the deficiency of the other. It comes as an equal shock to reflect that Congreve, whom we associate with Restoration drama, was nine years *younger* than Defoe, whom we associate with the eighteenth-century novel. But we shall be justified in using Congreve rather than Pope as the measure of what Defoe could not compass. The matter presents itself to me best in

[1] p. 145.   [2] pp. 105-6.

terms of flexibility and rigidity. It is not that Defoe had a rigid mind. On the contrary, Sutherland is right in speaking of his puckish spirit in his satire, the *Consolidator:*

> Defoe was the awkward boy who will persist in asking questions; the difference is that he knew quite well that he was being awkward . . . A bourgeois who delights to *épater les bourgeois*.[1]

Nevertheless, Defoe cannot overcome the rigidity of his given material. If he is to remain true to his choric task (a task of course not consciously conceived as such) of voicing the dissenting habit of mind, he cannot be too critical, he must identify himself with it. And the type of religion in question with its simple elections, interventions, rewards, admonitions, and punishments, and the type of mercantile morality in question with its surface justice and its ruthless self-seeking, could not be made flexible by however sensitive and imaginative an observer. Congreve's Mirabel and Millamant, with their affectations of frivolity and heartlessness advanced to screen much seriousness and warmth of feeling, betoken a world where mind can move with greater freedom, between more distant extremes. Defoe has his advantages. He can oscillate between present and past, between actual contemporary people and mankind in abstraction or mankind in a primitive phase of culture; but within his own contemporary province his oscillations are a good deal more confined. The styles of the two authors, so well attuned to their substance, confirm the contrast. Defoe's simplicity can compass the homeliness of the day and the timelessness of abstracted human nature but it lacks the subtle elegance, the diversified tempo, and the overtones and undertones of Congreve. This comparison is not a complaint that Defoe was not other than he was; it merely attempts to point out that however much we like Defoe and feel enthusiastically about him we must avoid the temptation of inflating his genius. I believe *Robinson Crusoe* to be an epic, but an epic having some of the limitations of the middle-class ethos whose choric expression it was.

[1] *Defoe*, p. 143.

3

'Tom Jones'

(i)

ON the surface *Tom Jones* looks more like being a prose epic than *Robinson Crusoe*. It derives from the heroic tradition, its author considered it such ("this heroic, historical, prosaic poem"), and later writers have been prone to support him. If, in the end, I decide against it as an epic in the sense I use the word, I should do so with reluctance and only after fair consideration of the other opinion.

(ii) *Inherited Character*

Those writers on *Tom Jones* with whom I am acquainted hardly make enough of its inherited constituents. They prefer the forward to the backward look and like to see it (as most people see the *Canterbury Tales*) as the great source from which later glory is derived; just as admirers of Manet's *Le Déjeuner sur l'herbe* are more apt to think of it as new in its day than as deriving from a painting of Giorgione in the Louvre. But neither the frock-coats in *Le Déjeuner* nor the references to the Methodists in *Tom Jones* alter the traditional features of the two works of art. Fielding himself admits his inheritance (see his preface to *Joseph Andrews*) and likes to think that the serious comic novel (serious as against the burlesque) went back to the lost *Margites* of Homer and that the great Renaissance prose romances are heroic poems either of the tragic or the comic variety. While Fénelon's *Télémaque* is the only successful specimen in the recent non-comic variety, the Scudéry type of romance still belongs to it. On the comic side, the great example is *Don Quixote*, of which Fielding declares *Joseph Andrews* to be an imitation. Thus, however much he knew he was an innovator, Fielding was at one with the most correct Augustan opinion in aiming at a wealth of classic precedent.[1] I will give a few instances of this aim, for it has been too little heeded.

The burlesque Homeric descriptions and similes in *Tom Jones*, however alien to our taste, force themselves on our notice; but they should count for much less than Fielding's consistent (and often tacit) loyalty to the long tradition of the medieval and Renaissance romance of chivalry. And even these similes glance simultaneously at *Télémaque*, which naturalised in its prose the poetical similes of Homer with conspicuous success; they are linked with the long European tradition. Then take Tom Jones himself. His setting is modern enough, but Fielding intended him for a real hero in the line of the heroes of chivalry. Digeon[2] may be right in saying that Tom's defenceless simplicity derives from *Gil Blas*, but this derivation does not alter, rather it serves to make credible, a character of an older ancestry. Early in the book Sophia asks Tom a favour; and he pledges himself instantly to grant it, "for by this dear hand I would sacrifice my life to oblige you". This is hardly strict realism in the modern manner, but neither is it thoughtless, provincial convention. On the contrary, Tom, offering his life, has an ancestry, deriving from the medieval knight who pledges himself to serve the commands of his lady. And for the rest of the book he is the knight-errant of romance and fairy-tale who wins his love after banishment, many adventures, and much misunderstanding. The knight must have a squire, and in due course Tom acquires Partridge, a character of the Cervantes breed, but none the less a comic version of a stock romance figure. Fielding of course keeps the heroic side of Tom well damped down in accord with his comic intentions; and withholds his full revelation of Tom's knightly appearance and aristocratic charm till half-way through the book. But soon after Tom's arrival at the inn at Upton (the scene of the story's most elaborate and thrilling complications) occurs his picture, which culminates in the pronouncement that

[1] Arthur L. Cooke in his article, 'Fielding and Writers of Heroic Romance', in *Publications of the Modern Language Association*, 1947, shows that, however different their results, the French writers of the prose heroic tale and Fielding worked on the same critical presuppositions.

[2] A. Digeon, *The Novels of Fielding* (London 1925), p. 144.

his face had a delicacy in it almost inexpressible, and which might have given him an air rather too effeminate, had it not been joined to a most masculine person and mien; which latter had as much in them of the Hercules, as the former had of the Adonis.

When, later, he learns that Sophia too has been at the inn unknown to him and that he and Partridge have not the means of pursuing her, he falls into a mad fury:

> "Cruel Sophia! Cruel! No. Let me blame myself—No, let me blame thee. D—nation seize thee, fool, blockhead! thou hast undone me, and I will tear thy soul from thy body."—At which words he laid violent hands on the collar of poor Partridge, and shook him more heartily than an ague fit, or his own fears, had ever done before.[1]

And though Fielding soon interrupts his account of Jones "playing the madman for many minutes" with the remark that if he took pains to elaborate it the reader would not reciprocate those pains in the perusal, he means us to think of Ariosto and of Jones as an Orlando, *furioso* at the loss of his mistress.

Nor are the echoes of the heroic romances confined to the hero. The fight at the end of the fifth book between Thwackum and Blifil on the one side and Tom Jones on the other repeats the motive of the good knight-errant attacked by two bad men: a motive made more traditional still by the intervention of a fourth knight, Mr Western. The delightful comic scene (XII, p. 5), where the drumming that reaches the ears of Tom and Partridge turns out to come not, as they feared, from soldiers but from a puppet-show, is pure and unabashed *Don Quixote*. Allworthy is derived in part from Eubulus in Sidney's *Arcadia*; and his visit to London late in the book duplicates Eubulus's arrival in *Arcadia* to dispense justice all round.

It is by such means that Fielding, throughout *Tom Jones*, conveys the kind of sentiment that Milton conveyed when he called the 'argument' of *Paradise Lost*

> Not less but more Heroic than the wrauth
> Of stern *Achilles* on his Foe pursu'd
> Thrice Fugitive about *Troy* Wall;

[1] XII, p. 3.

or that Spenser conveyed when, opening the *Faerie Queene*, he echoed, in "Lo! I, the man whose Muse whylome . . .", the exordium of the *Aeneid*. Fielding, of course, does not, like Spenser and Milton, declare frank competition; he says rather, "In this deliberately toned down romance, which substitutes a natural for the high heroic theme, I am still in the heroic tradition and claim to compete with my predecessors. Homer wrote his comic *Margites*; and if it were discovered, *Don Quixote* would be found its worthiest recent successor, as *Jerusalem Delivered* is that of the *Iliad*. My romance belongs to this comic branch of the heroic tradition."

If these were Fielding's conscious aims, we should give every consideration to the chance that in his masterpiece he achieved an epic.

(iii) *Critics' Opinions*

Fielding's conception of the comic epic found support in the eighteenth century. For instance, Lord Monboddo, in his *Of the Origin and Progress of Language*, echoed Fielding's claim in the preface to *Joseph Andrews*:

> There is lately sprung up among us a species of narrative poem, representing likewise (*sc.* like comedy) the characters of common life. It has the same relation to comedy that the epic has to tragedy, and differs from the epic in the same respect that comedy differs from tragedy; that is, in the actions and characters, both of which are much nobler in the epic than in it. It is therefore a legitimate kind of poem.[1]

And Monboddo adds that *Tom Jones* with its living characters is its great English example. Later he applies an Aristotelian criterion to the book and finds its surpassing merit in the management of the 'fable'. Every incident contributes to one end, and the various turns of fortune give delight.

> And, therefore, as I hold the invention and composition of the fable to be the chief beauty of every poem, I must be of opinion that Mr Fielding was one of the greatest poetical geniuses of his age; nor do I think that his work has hitherto met with the praise that it deserves.[2]

[1] Vol. 3 (Edinburgh 1776), p. 134.   [2] *Ib.*, p. 298, note.

In the present century, too, critics have hailed *Tom Jones* as epic. Orlo Williams finds it the best-balanced and most comprehensive of the novels:

> Fielding was happy when he wrote it, not yet overburdened in body or mind by his work as a magistrate, and he appeared to have a firm grasp of life in all its essentials.

Fielding, he says, writes as it were from an eminence:

> To the epic or comic poet a pinnacle of this kind is necessary; like Homer, he must know how the gods laugh over their banquet on Olympus when they observe the antics of puny mortals. Yet only the power of his own mind, not the gods themselves, will so lift him up; and he who tries to fly without the wings comes down like Icarus. Fielding had the wings, and, when he wrote *Tom Jones*, he sat laughing with the gods. There is something superhuman, almost inhuman, in utterances of comedy when supreme upon the heights, but they are comprehensive and compelling.[1]

However different his way of writing, Orlo Williams is here saying the sort of thing that Monboddo and Fielding himself had said. My final citation claims epic quality for *Tom Jones* in terms that come near the conception of the epic I have made the ground of this book. It is from Digeon's *Novels of Fielding*.

> All works . . . which deserve to be called 'Epics' express, at a given moment, the soul of a generation, in all its fullness and all its depth, perhaps in all the dimness of its hidden dream. . . . A work is epic when it is the complete expression of a moment of collective life, a fragment of the legend of the centuries. . . . The individuality of the author is drowned in a sort of mass-personality; the voice of a whole people speaks through his voice.

Like *Gargantua* and *Don Quixote*, *Tom Jones* is epic in this sense: "*Tom Jones* is the England of the time."[2]

(iv) *Epic or Not?*

Is then *Tom Jones* an epic in effect as well as in profession? There is no doubt about its 'Englishness'; but Englishness

---

[1] *Some Great English Novelists* (London 1926), pp. 23-4.
[2] pp. 179-80.

need not be the same as "expressing the soul of a generation" of English life. Take the cases of Sidney and Trollope. If you look closely at *Arcadia*, you will find certain English character-istics; for instance near the beginning Kalander's house is, in its architecture, local and not Continental: but *Arcadia* is stronger in expressing the soul of the Elizabethan age than in enveloping you in the actual life of the country and thus in creating a dominant impression of its Englishness. With Trol-lope the reverse is true. He fairly envelops you in the life of the country; he makes you wallow in it; and you ask no better: but as for expressing the soul of a generation in all its depth, no, that is a thing we should not dream of expecting from Trollope. The question is: does Fielding in *Tom Jones* join the qualities of Sidney to those of Trollope?

Taking for granted that *Tom Jones* impresses us with its Englishness, giving convincing pictures of the English scene and of much English life, we may concede that through its politics, its awareness of the Methodists and even its passing references to the music of Handel it goes beyond the bounds of the pure comedy of manners. Fielding was a sincere Whig, believing in the revolution of 1688 and the Hanoverian succession. Before beginning *Tom Jones* he had pamphleteered vigorously against the Stuarts and in support of the House of Hanover.[1] And through this active part in the struggle he was later able to impart an uncommon life to the political setting, that of the '45, which he chose for the main action of his novel. Not that the political references cover many pages, but they make their impression; they vouch for a breadth of interest; they add a new dimension to the work. On the other hand, though the mere observation of the Methodists may be better than none at all, its superficiality points to what Fielding lacked, namely the entry into the whole world of Defoe. Defoe's world was a cruder and in some ways a narrower one. But there was new life in it and more of a stir than in the rural depths of western England and an uncommercial section of London society. Defoe touched the more dynamic portion of the age. However, no one man could have grasped all the disparities of

[1] For this see, for instance, Wilbur L. Cross, *The History of Henry Fielding* (New Haven 1918), ii. p. 14 ff.

early and mid eighteenth-century England; and Fielding may have grasped enough for the purposes of an epic. He may have grasped as much (though the ingredients were different) as Gibbon; and Gibbon through the *Decline and Fall of the Roman Empire* delivered, in his way, the belated epic of the 1688 revolution.[1]

That Fielding controlled his material is beyond doubt. Orlo Williams's talk about the pinnacle and the top of Olympus is justified. I cannot indeed join the chorus of praise, led by Lord Monboddo, for the perfect way *Tom Jones* is plotted. There is too much plot, too many surprising turns. These end by wearying; and most wearisome of all is the last major turn, of Tom thinking he has committed incest with his mother: a gratuitous complication dragged in when we are sated and want the book to finish. Nevertheless, whether or not he lacked tact, Fielding was in control from beginning to end, as much as Thackeray in *Vanity Fair* and Meredith in the *Egoist*. But there are degrees of control, degrees of the imaginative pressure on the material to hand. At times that pressure can be intense. Take Sophia's letter to Tom (in VI, p. 13) telling him she will not submit to marry Blifil:

> Sir,—It is impossible to express what I have felt since I saw you. Your submitting, on my account, to such cruel insults from my father, lays me under an obligation I shall ever own. As you know his temper, I beg you will, for my sake, avoid him. I wish I had any comfort to send you; but believe this, that nothing but the last violence shall ever give my hand or heart where you would be sorry to see them bestowed.

Fielding has there done the supremely difficult thing of finding the right words at the moment of high passion. All Sophia's good breeding, delicate feeling, resolution, and warmth of heart are distilled into these few words. Only an intense exercise of the imagination could have found them. Again, the incident of Sophia leaving her muff (which has already figured large in the book) in the bed to be occupied by Tom and Mrs Waters and of his discovering it too late is, in its own and different way, equally intense. Even in his moralising, where

[1] See E. M. W. Tillyard, *The English Epic and its Background*, pp. 510-27.

intensity is least to be expected, Fielding can surprise and compel, as where he assures us that Sophia was less upset at Tom's having gone to bed with Mrs Waters than at his having (as she wrongly thought) made free with her name and condition among the company in the inn parlour. And Fielding crowns the consistently splendid comedy of Squire Western and his sister, their disputes and reconciliations, his violent manner and his secret fear of her, with the grand surprise, for which we are quite unprepared, of a really serious breach. That surprise is imagined with uncommon intensity.

Other examples of comparable intensity could probably be found; indeed the whole chain of the events that take place at the inn at Upton is intensely imagined. Yet on the whole the vision of the novelist from his Olympus is not so much intense as leisured, kindly, and critical; a vision that observes and records with consummate skill and admirable sympathy but which transmutes only at exceptional moments. Take the hero and set him alongside Crusoe. We learn as much about his mind as we do of Crusoe's; and yet never for an instant does he turn into a symbolic figure, an Everyman, as Crusoe does. He remains a likable and adequate comic hero. I make these comparisons not because I wish to argue that *Tom Jones* is a worse novel than *Robinson Crusoe* but in order to make clear a certain element that *Tom Jones* lacks.

Tom Jones, then, lacks sustained intensity; it does not make the heroic impression; and on that account it fails of the epic effect. And Fielding's claim to be in the tradition of the comic epic can in no way influence this conclusion. Not that such a conclusion affects the success of *Tom Jones*; it merely warns us what *Tom Jones* is not. Take *Tom Jones* as a comedy in the form of a narrative fiction, reflecting the manners rather than the soul of a generation, and you find its success beyond doubt and its merits worthy of the praise which has greeted it since its birth.

4

Scott

(i) General and Historical

ALTHOUGH Defoe had the advantage over Fielding in being familiar with the most vigorous and creative part of English society, he was less fortunate than Scott, who was born into a nation both full of a youthful vigour and unafflicted by the kind of social divisions that prevailed in England. The changes that took place in Scotland during the eighteenth century were shared by every class; the heightening of vitality was spread so fairly that the danger of jealousy, strong when a single section of the community waxes in power and prosperity, simply did not arise. Landowners, professional men, tradesmen, mechanics, peasants were all better off and held their heads higher at the end of the eighteenth century than at the beginning. And if the more romantic Scotsmen lamented that the relics of an unnaturally surviving feudalism had to be sacrificed in the process and if a few Highland chieftains thought more money and a less precarious life an ignoble recompense for the loss of feudal power, the overwhelming conviction (comprehending romantics as well as realists) was that Scotland had come into her own.

G. M. Trevelyan sums up the great revival as follows:

For a generation or more, the benefits of the Union seemed to hang fire. But after the liquidation of the Jacobite and Highland questions in 1745-1746, Scotland sprang forward along the path towards happier days. Her agriculture, which had been to the last degree antiquated and miserable, could, before the Century closed, give lessons to the improving landlords of England. Scottish farmers, gardeners, engineers and doctors came south and taught the English many things. Englishmen began to travel in Scotland and to admire both her mountains and her men. Scots took a large share in the commerce and colonization of the British Empire, in the wars of Britain, in the government of India.

Released from the prison of poverty where she had languished for ages, Scotland burst into sudden splendour. Her religion lost much of its gloom and fanaticism, while remaining vital and democratic. The genius of her sons gave a lead to the thought of the world. Hume, Adam Smith, Robertson, Dugald Stewart, extended their influence not only over all Britain but into the salons of continental philosophers, while Smollett, Boswell and Burns made their native country famous in letters, and Raeburn in art. Thus the latter part of the Eighteenth Century saw the golden age of Scotland, which was prolonged for a second generation of glory when Sir Walter, with his lays and romances, imposed the Scottish idea upon all Europe.[1]

It is true that Scotland had no separate political life, but, to quote Trevelyan again,

Politics are not everything. The social, imaginative and intellectual life of the land of Burns and Scott was vigorous in inverse proportion to the political atrophy.[2]

Add to this that Scotland was forward also in developing industry. As early as 1760 were founded the Carron iron works between Edinburgh and Stirling, where iron-ore, coal, and water-power were available in the same place.

This prosperity and sense of national well-being at the turn of the centuries was one thing that held Scotsmen together. Another was the traditional adjustment of the different classes: an adjustment peculiar to Scotland. Although the Scottish peasantry at the beginning of the eighteenth century still lived in a state of feudal submission to their lairds, they retained a freedom of speech and of intercourse with their superiors unenjoyed by the corresponding class in England. The special reasons, apart from the native independence of the Scottish character, were the power of the Church and the habits of education. Kirk Session and Presbytery, representing the humble classes, were bold in criticising the nobility, in a way that astonished even Nonconformist visitors from England. The village school provided education for the laird's sons as well as for the other boys.

[1] G. M. Trevelyan, *English Social History* (London 1944), pp. 418-19.
[2] *Ib.*, p. 458.

The idea of sending a Scottish gentleman's son to an English public school was rendered unthinkable alike by thrift and by patriotism. Education in the village school strengthened the young laird's love of his native land and landscape, and inclined him when he came to man's estate to sympathy with his tenants who had once been his schoolfellows. The broad Scots tongue, of which the highest were not ashamed, the traditions and ballads of the countryside, were the common heritage of all.[1]

The sum of all these conditions was that a single temper animated the whole country, offering to the creative writer a potentiality of epic effect that simply did not exist in the neighbouring country of England.

Of course, such a single temper need not mean absence of conflict. Peasants in Lowlands and gillies in Highlands might use a common familiarity of speech with their betters; but it does not follow that there was no hostility between Highland and Lowland. The Union may have brought England and Scotland closer; and the great majority of Scotsmen may have recognised the consequent benefits: but it does not follow that England and Scotland saw eye to eye. Merchants and farming lairds may have enjoyed a common prosperity; but it does not follow that town and country were loving neighbours. But the old conflicts were no longer fatal; they spelt rivalry and competition and not destruction. Making for variety and against a lazy uniformity, they gave the creative writer the kind of scope he needed. In a few of his novels Scott made use of that scope.

(ii) *Scott and Scotsmen*

No one of Scott's novels can be called an epic, but his early novels dealing with recent or fairly recent Scottish life and history form what I have called elsewhere an 'epic area'.[2] In using the phrase I like to have a physical metaphor in view. Just as there exist volcanic areas containing many eruptions of boiling mud or steaming water but no undoubted volcano, so you can have a literary area favourable to epic but not producing one undoubted specimen. Such was the great age

[1] *Ib.*, p. 426.　　　　[2] *English Epic*, pp. 124, 126, 260.

in Iceland, where no one saga topped the rest; such was the age of Elizabeth, which in Shakespeare's History Plays, the *Faerie Queene*, and *Arcadia*, produced three important, yet imperfect, epic attempts. I shall plead that within the general 'epic area' of Scott's early Scottish novels three stand out as nearer to epic success than the rest.

Going on to describe Scott's 'epic area' I will begin symbolically, taking as my paradigm his monument in Edinburgh. This, in its isolated Neo-Gothicism, is pitifully inadequate, representing no more than the *Talisman* side of Scott and his more melodramatic heroes and villains. But as a point of union between the old Edinburgh, severely yet romantically dominated by its castle, and the squares and terraces of the eighteenth-century city, and as roughly the centre of the alien visitors' excursions, it implies vastly more than its inadequate self. It implies a new creation embracing and harmonising the old and the new elements, a creation approved by many people and a source of legitimate local pride.

To use the Scott monument thus is to repeat the assertions of his orthodox critics. John Buchan said that Scott "had the good fortune to stand at the meeting-place of two worlds and to have it in him to be their chief interpreter".[1] Grierson pointed out Scott's office as the great reconciler: he reconciled Highlands and Lowlands, Celt and Angle. "He even helped to reconcile Britain to the continent and the continent to Britain after the long years of exile and isolation." And within his own nation he reconciled the different classes, the rich and the poor.[2] Further, Scotsmen owe their character in the eyes of other people to Scott in the first place.[3]

If the orthodox critics are right, if the best of the Waverley Novels served and represented their country in such a way, I can hardly be wrong in calling these novels an 'epic area'.

But we cannot leave matters thus. Younger Scotsmen than Buchan and Grierson have had other opinions. Take the gloomy surmises of Edwin Muir that, for all his greatness, Scott

[1] John Buchan, *Sir Walter Scott* (London 1932), p. 43.
[2] H. J. C. Grierson, 'Scott and Carlyle', in *Essays and Studies of the English Association*, 1928, pp. 104-5.
[3] *Ib.*, p. 107.

is empty because there was a void at the centre of Scottish national life. Scottish literature, he remarks, lost its independence in the seventeenth century with the result that "what traditional value Scott's work possessed was at second hand, and derived mainly from English literature, which he knew intimately but which was a semi-foreign literature to him". Without a continuous tradition and an assured centre of national life, "Scott can find a real image of Scotland only in the past". His mind is divided in its loyalty to the present fact of the Union and to the old independent Scotland. And Muir contrasts Fielding, who, by no means a greater writer, scores by living in an organic society.[1] Muir's picture of Scott excludes all notion of reconciliation.

These are delicate matters for an Englishman to meddle with. But surely the predicament which Muir describes is not entirely Scottish: it was common to the whole of the British Isles at the time of the two great revolutions, French and industrial. Burke was as much upset that the age of chivalry was past as Scott was that there was no more sense in the old Highland ways of life. Peacock was equally alive to the price that had to be paid for so-called progress. In the matter of rhetoric, I cannot see that Scott was troubled by the lack of a tradition of polite Scots prose, for there had been enough good Scottish writers of English prose before him to tame and domesticate the English tradition. Scott is utterly at ease in the prose idiom of Augustan Britain from Congreve and Dryden to Hume, as much so as in the Scottish vernacular he used for a great part of his dialogue. When he writes ill, the badness has nothing to do with the lack of a Scottish tradition; it is the badness to which the English tradition was naturally prone.

To Englishmen, Muir's complaint about the lack of a national centre seems strange, for they are continually struck by the success with which Scotsmen keep their national character. And when one of them, David Cecil, compares Fielding with Scott, it is to say that while most of Fielding's characters could be transplanted to another land or century without thereby being destroyed, Scott's best characters are

[1] Edwin Muir, *Scott and Scotland* (London 1936), pp. 11-12, 127, 140, 145.

so ingrained with Scottishness that transplantation would be the end of them.[1] Muir, therefore, does not convince me.

On the other hand, it is a serious matter indeed if, as seems the case, the present generation of Scotsmen find that the Waverley Novels do not ring their bell. It suggests that their former epic character has not stood the test of time; and it demands that a critic today should not just accept the prevailing orthodoxy (whether or not he is in temperamental sympathy with it) but should once more put the old questions with a mind unprejudiced as to what the answers will turn out to be.

(iii) *Need for Re-assessment*

(a) *In General*

Trying to recollect the reputation of the different Waverley Novels in England fifty years ago, when I was first in process of reading them, I retain the impression that *Ivanhoe* was considered the masterpiece, with the *Talisman* nearly as good. I refer to the common not to the most refined or the academic opinion. Since then there has been a change; and even the common opinion has begun to admit that Scott's best novels (with the possible exception of *Redgauntlet*) were the first, and that he should be judged by these. There have been different reasons for such discrimination. Mario Praz[2] prefers the early Scott because only there do you find those descriptions of homely life, those *genre* or *Biedermeier* scenes, that Scott excels in. This is a perfectly good reason; but to centre *all* Scott's excellence in *Biedermeier* is to rush to an extreme nearly as false as the old one of making *Ivanhoe* the masterpiece. And I agree with those who think the early novels best for more than one reason; for including the freshest adventure and the deepest felt political opinions along with the most convincing pictures of social life.

Having agreed with modern orthodoxy that the novels of Scott that mainly matter are the first seven—*Waverley*, *Guy Mannering*, the *Antiquary*, *Old Mortality*, *Rob Roy*, the *Heart of*

---

[1] Lord David Cecil, *Sir Walter Scott* (London 1933), pp. 4-5.
[2] In the *Hero in Eclipse in Victorian Fiction* (London 1956).

Midlothian, and the *Bride of Lammermoor*—plus *Redgauntlet*, I have to differ from certain opinions on them by writers who, by nationality or length of study, should be better judges than I am. First, and generally, I find more fluctuation of quality within the list than is usually found, which makes me suspect that the novels which compose it have still not been read closely enough, that they still need re-assessment. Secondly, I keep challenging much usual opinion on details. For instance, Grierson endorses the old notion (put forward by James Ballantyne when the manuscript of *Waverley* was submitted to him) that the first chapters are long-winded and contribute little to the understanding of the hero's character. On the contrary, they are beautifully timed and they build up successfully the character of the only hero Scott chose to depict in any great detail. John Buchan calls Waverley "the average educated Englishman". On the contrary, Waverley is far too imaginative and impressionable to be anything of the sort. David Cecil denies proportion to *Waverley* and *Rob Roy*. On the contrary, they are the best contrived and plotted of all the Scottish novels. Daiches notes the speed and deftness and the truth to character displayed in the first letters of *Redgauntlet*. On the contrary, parts of them show Scott at his heaviest and dreariest: their archness is so clumsy that I am ashamed for the author, while the characterisation is painfully obvious and ingenuous. I carp in this manner not because I think these critics have written ill on Scott—no, they have written very well—but in order to reinforce my plea that even by this time Scott has not been read closely enough, that the discrimination to which I have referred has not gone far enough, that readers of Scott have oversimplified him and have read his best work too much influenced by the inferior, that they have not been sufficiently prepared for surprises, and that they have sometimes taken him not as he comes but as they have decided to think he will come. Hence, for instance, the error of thinking the opening chapters of *Waverley* long-winded.

I am forced to extend my carping to certain passages in Scott habitually chosen for special praise. These are, I should guess, Jeanie Deans's speech to Queen Anne in supplication for her sister's life (the *Heart of Midlothian*), Meg Merrilies's speech to the Laird of Ellangowan when the gipsies are being evicted from his estate (*Guy Mannering*), and Claverhouse's speech to Morton on glory (*Old Mortality*). With the praise given to the first passage I can go all the way; about the other two I feel more coolly.

Here is a part of Meg's speech with the two preceding paragraphs to give the setting:

> She was standing upon one of those high banks, which, as we before noticed, overhung the road; so that she was placed considerably higher than Ellangowan, even though he was on horseback; and her tall figure, relieved against the clear blue sky, seemed almost of supernatural height. We have noticed, that there was in her general attire, or rather in her mode of adjusting it, somewhat of a foreign costume, artfully adopted perhaps for the purpose of adding to the effect of her spells and predictions, or perhaps from some traditional notions respecting the dress of her ancestors. On this occasion, she had a large piece of red cotton cloth rolled about her head in the form of a turban, from beneath which her dark eyes flashed with uncommon lustre. Her long and tangled black hair fell in elf-locks from the folds of this singular head-gear. Her attitude was that of a sybil in frenzy, and she stretched out, in her right hand, a sapling bough which seemed just pulled.
>
> "I'll be d—d," said the groom, "if she has not been cutting the young ashes in the Dukit park."—The Laird made no answer, but continued to look at the figure which was thus perched above his path.
>
> "Ride your ways," said the gypsey, "ride your ways, Laird of Ellangowan—ride your ways, Godfrey Bertram!—This day have ye quenched seven smoking hearths—see if the fire in your ain parlour burn the blither for that. Ye have riven the thack off seven cottar houses—look if your ain roof-tree stand the faster.— Ye may stable your stirks in the shealings at Derncleugh—see that the hare does not couch on the hearthstane at Ellangowan."

What I cannot get over here is the coolness with which Scott makes his preparations. He has leisure to correct Meg's "general attire" to "her mode of adjusting it", and to wonder why she adopted that mode: whether "for the purpose of adding to the effect of her spells" or "from some traditional notions respecting the dress of her ancestors"—these two last phrases being in themselves well calculated to damp any sense of urgency and excitement. The picture is perfectly clear, but there are no surprising collocations of words that could add interest to clarity or excitement to Scott's leisurely method. "Her dark eyes flashed with uncommon lustre" and "Her long and tangled black hair fell in elf-locks" might have occurred in a dozen Novels of Terror written by authors very inferior to Scott. The word "perched", suggesting a bird's crouched attitude, contradicts the towering figure Meg is supposed to present. As a result of such cool leisure and mediocrity of language I am unprepared for the balanced, incantatory sentence-structure and the strong alliteration of the speech itself. Instead of being deeply poetical, pathetic, and of fitting the gypsies' unhappy plight and Ellangowan's tragic folly, it becomes something contrived, a piece of rhetoric put into the mouth of a stagey character, not issuing from the inmost being of a real and suffering woman. In this scene Meg Merrilies belongs not to the company of living characters in fiction (so many of whom Scott himself created) but to the melodramatic crew that people the Neo-Gothic novel and the verse narratives of Lord Byron.

Claverhouse's speech to Morton ("But, in truth, Mr Morton, why should we care so much for death . . .") is a much finer affair, a noble and fascinating piece of rhetoric that bears much re-reading. And yet when we measure it by a truly great rendering of the same heroic creed, for instance Sarpedon's words to Glaucus in the twelfth book of the *Iliad* (whether in the original or in Pope's version beginning, "Why boast we, Glaucus, our extended reign"), we find that it does not reach the depths of our nature, we fail to identify ourselves with Claverhouse but, having come near, pause and then salute him from a little distance.

To make the same point, but from the reverse direction, I will pass to a passage from *Waverley* which, though less ambitious than the two passages I have cited, is not only more successful but concerns areas of the mind Scott is supposed to have little to do with. It is the end of the fifty-second chapter and it consists of a conversation between Flora Mac-Ivor and Rose Bradwardine about Waverley. The time is after the Battle of Prestonpans and before the rebels have left Edinburgh on their march to Derby. Flora has rejected Waverley's advances more than once and, mindful of what Jane Austen calls the "duty of woman to woman", is working to get his affections transferred from herself to Rose. She is doing them both a kindness, and with a good will, yet, with her personal pride and Jacobite fanaticism, she cannot but despise them in her heart. She complains that Waverley's zeal is frozen by the proud cold-blooded Englishman (Waverley's prisoner at Prestonpans) whom he now lives with so much; and the dialogue continues, beginning with Rose's answer:

> "Colonel Talbot—he is a very disagreeable person to be sure. He looks as if he thought no Scottish woman worth the trouble of handing her a cup of tea. But Waverley is so gentle, so well informed—"
>
> "Yes, he can admire the moon, and quote a stanza from Tasso."
>
> "Besides, you know how he fought."
>
> "For mere fighting," answered Flora, "I believe all men (that is, who deserve the name) are pretty much alike: there is generally more courage required to run away. They have besides, when confronted with each other, a certain instinct for strife, as we see in other male animals, such as dogs, bulls, and so forth. But high and perilous enterprize is not Waverley's forte. He would never have been his celebrated ancestor Sir Nigel, but only Sir Nigel's eulogist and poet. I will tell you where he will be at home, my dear, and in his place,—in the quiet circle of domestic happiness, lettered indolence, and elegant enjoyments of Waverley-Honour. And he will refit the old library in the most exquisite Gothic taste, and garnish its shelves with the rarest and most valuable volumes;—and he will draw plans and landscapes, and write verses, and rear temples, and dig grottoes;—and he will stand in a clear summer night in the colonnade before the hall, and gaze on the deer as they stray in the moonlight, or lie shadowed by the boughs of the huge old fantastic oaks;—and he will repeat verses to his beautiful wife, who shall hang upon his arm;—and he will be a happy man."
>
> "And she will be a happy woman," thought poor Rose. But she only sighed, and dropped the conversation.

If Meg Merrilies was melodramatic and if we just stop short of identifying ourselves with Claverhouse, Flora speaks in flawless accord with her complicated character and we have immediate access into it. The Novel of Terror might never have existed, for the passage is in the purest strain of eighteenth-century irony and sophistication. And yet the description of the moonlight at Waverley-Honour, which Flora puts to an ironic—even fiercely ironic—use, is very lovely; and we are perfectly free to apprehend the irony and the beauty at the same time. Indeed, Flora speaks with the accent of one of Congreve's heroines. Her language, though not striking or obtrusive, is perfectly chosen. Nothing could be more delicate than the way she uses the future tense in "and he will repeat verses to his beautiful wife, who shall hang upon his arm". Flora keeps on with 'will' in referring to Waverley, for she is serenely, even boredly, certain of *his* destined life: but who his wife will be is not yet certain; and Flora gently insists that it must be a loving and a clinging one, in fact none other than Rose, so that *shall* not *will* is the appropriate form of the future tense. Nothing, too, could be more apt than the verbs in "draw plans and landscapes, and write verses, and rear temples, and dig grottoes". Though so easily and quietly done the writing is intense.

Now, finished irony and intense writing are things we have been taught *not* to expect in Scott. It is time we cultivated a wiser passiveness in reading him and a less stereotyped set of expectations.

(b) *Variation of Tempo*

One reason why there has been too little discrimination in reading Scott's novels is that it is assumed that they all demand the same speed of reading. He stands uniformly as the essentially narrative novelist whom you have to read briskly for the sake of following closely the interest of the story. Such assumptions work very well for the *Talisman* and for a number of other Waverley Novels. Thus taken and not required to reveal any depth of moral truth or any subtly or passionately conceived characters, the *Talisman* could not be bettered. It is full of stir and colour and it achieves the simple ends of amusing the reader and quickening his pulse. That was what Scott meant it to do, and the reader should be content to take the book as Scott meant it. But try to read *Waverley* or the *Heart of*

Midlothian at a speed suited to the *Talisman,* and you end in confusion. Avid for the story, you find the opening of *Waverley* dull, missing its reflective deliberateness, and the opening of the *Heart of Midlothian* clotted through the introduction of two apparently or only forcedly related topics: the Porteous Riots and the fortunes of the Deans family. Sometimes, it is true, Scott is uncertain of himself, and it is impossible to gauge the proper speed: deliberate and mellow comedy will demand one speed, and a conventional and heartless complication of plot or an arbitrary intrusion of romantic improbability will demand another. The reader will just have to come to terms with the different modes as best he may, and he cannot escape discomfort in the process. The one right principle is to have no prejudices and to be ready for anything.

(c) *Unusual Habits of Composition*

In pleading that the Waverley Novels should be read with fresh eyes and re-assessed I would point not only to the variations of tempo in them but to the strangeness of Scott's habits as an author. There is a story in Lockhart's Life about the way he composed three of his novels when he was suffering from cramp in the stomach. One of these was the *Bride of Lammermoor.* Most of this, according to Lockhart, Scott dictated from a sofa:

> But when dialogue of peculiar animation was in progress, spirit seemed to triumph altogether over matter—he arose from his couch and walked up and down the room, raising and lowering his voice, and as if he were acting the parts.

When the novel was finished and "was first put into his hand in a complete shape, he did not recollect one single incident, character, or conversation it contained". Unluckily, Lockhart was wrong about the dictation, for most of the manuscript of the *Bride of Lammermoor* survives in Scott's own hand.[1] But both parts of Lockhart's story, true to fact or not, testify correctly to the vehemence with which Scott composed and to the completeness with which he shed, one could almost say disowned, the children of his brain, once they were born. It is the

[1] See H. J. C. Grierson, *Sir Walter Scott, Bart.,* pp. 183-4.

combination of the two things that is so queer. In spite of the demonic energy with which he composed, Scott's references in his letters to his artistic creation are few, casual, and short. Tree-planting, moving house, other authors, advice to a friend on melancholia, archaeology, dinner with Royalty are all more weighty matters than his own writing. One reason for thus scaling his interests was that he heartily accepted the pre-Romantic faith that art, however great, must be subordinate to the greater art of living. It was the faith that persuaded Milton to drop his epic ambitions for politics and Congreve to abandon authorship when he felt it to compromise his integrity as a gentleman; and it is allied to the faith in the social obligation of the artist, whose duty was to serve his public and not merely to please himself. His public's pleasure was a part of general life as his own private satisfaction was not, and it had the prior claim. Believing thus, Scott thought it was the public rather than himself which should, if it wished, be voluble on his compositions. In this conflict between public demand and private desire the right principle is a compromise: right, because in the end it gives the best results. Scott is strange in the degree in which he yielded to public demand. I doubt if any major English writer went so far as he did.

Now, such extremity argues some unusual habit of mind; and John Buchan[1] may have identified it when he observed that Scott, for all his social ease and intense living, habitually fostered a secret life to which he could retire and about which he was almost silent—and, he might have added, of which he was afraid. Buchan associates it partly with his early love for Williamina Stuart-Belches, a thwarted one which (like Télémaque's for Eucharis) retained its clear impression through his life. But it included his congenital and never exhausted power of make-believe. Scott both portrayed and satirised his own castle-building passion through the character of Waverley. Waverley, a sensitive young man deprived of the society of his equals, indulged in romantic dreams. But he was terrified of revealing them:

So far was Edward Waverley from expecting general sympathy with his own feelings, or concluding that the present state of

[1] *Op. cit.*, p. 53 ff.

things was calculated to exhibit the reality of visions in which he loved to indulge, that he dreaded nothing more than the detection of such sentiments as were dictated by his musings. He neither had nor wished to have a confidant, with whom to communicate his reveries; and so sensible was he of the ridicule attached to them, that, had he been able to chuse between any punishment short of ignominy, and the necessity of giving a cold and composed account of the ideal world in which he lived the better part of his days, I think he would not have hesitated to chuse the former affliction.

Waverley represents only a part of Scott's character, and it was because of the unlikeness to the whole of him that Scott dares to betray through Waverley that secret life about which he was uneasy, even to the point of fear. For it is only through uneasiness and fear that I can account for the acerbity with which Scott attacked his hero:

> The heroe is a sneaking piece of imbecility and if he had married Flora she would have set him up upon the chimney-piece as Count Boralaski's wife used to do with him.[1]

What form the fear took can be gathered from his correspondence elsewhere. Writing to his young literary friend, Robert Gillies, in 1812, he deplores this friend's proneness to melancholy and gives his antidote:

> The fiend which haunts you is one who, if resisted, will flee from you. Plunge into active study, diversified by agreeable company, and regular exercise; ride, walk, dance or shoot, or hunt, or break stones on the highway rather than despond about your health, which is the surest way in the world to bring about the catastrophe which you are apprehensive of.[2]

And again:

> Active exertion is peremptorily imposed upon us as a law of our nature; and as the price of that degree of happiness, which our present state of existence admits of. You see the rich and the proud reduced to purchase contentment, and their night's rest by the hardest bodily labour. Those to whom nature has kindly

[1] *Letters of Sir Walter Scott 1811-14*, ed. H. J. C. Grierson (London 1932), p. 478. Joseph Borowlaski was a Polish dwarf.
[2] *Ib.*, p. 108.

indulged the power of literary labour, occupying the higher, instead of their mere corporeal functions, ought not surely to be less active in their pursuits than mere fishers or fox-hunters.[1]

What is interesting (and so characteristic of Scott as opposed to other great creative writers) is that the demon in question is merely the melancholy that comes from day-dreaming and indolence. He refuses to acknowledge the other demon dependent for its material on the day-dreaming faculty, the demon of imaginative creation, and classes the 'literary labour' with fishing and hunting, practical pursuits able to defeat the only demon he allows. It is an extraordinary refusal, for if any man has ever been exposed to the creative urge it is Scott. And the only way I can account for it is through fear. Thus he must never allow too much rein to the secret life of the fancy; such indulgence could only lead to the cold hillside to which Keats's Belle Dame betrayed the Knight. Scott had no faith in the mood of indolence through which Keats thought he could banish the vision of his demon, Poesy. So long as that demon provoked activity he could be indulged, but the moment a given spell of activity was completed he must be suppressed.

Scott's distrust of the creative urge is of a piece with his distrust of any indulgence of the passions. In this he is at complete odds with the greatest of his contemporary authors. It is the motive behind his very revealing comment on Byron, now in exile:

> What a pity that a man of such exquisite genius will not be con
> tented to be happy on the ordinary terms! I declare my heart
> bleeds for him when I think of him self-banished from the
> country to which he is an honour.[2]

It is also most revealing that, after the wonderful scene late in *Rob Roy* when Frank meets Diana and she kisses and leaves him as if for good, Frank is immediately ashamed of the outburst of passion he indulges in, recovers sooner than might be expected, and resumes his path *without giving himself time accurately to examine his motives*. It was his fear of indulging the demon when it had ceased to be useful that caused Scott both to

[1] *Ib.*, p. 120.   [2] *Letters*, ed. Grierson 1815-17, p. 319.

be unnaturally incurious of its nature and to forget the children of his brain, turning outwards from the *adytum* of that brain to all kinds of external activity. Luckily, his power of leaving and re-entering this *adytum* at short notice was astonishing: a contrast to Conrad's two years' absence from the external world when he wrote *Nostromo*.

The conclusion I wish to draw is that if Scott refused to examine the most powerful impulses of his brain he must have been singularly at their mercy when they were genuinely at work. We must expect a considerable waywardness of genius: yet one more reason why we should read unprejudiced, prepared for anything that turns up.

(iv) *The Three Epicising Novels*

Having pleaded that Scott should be reconsidered, I must go on to give the result of my own reconsideration. While I agree with Walter Allen that "Scott's Scottish novels coalesce in the mind into one great epic picture", and while I accept the list, given above, of the novels of Scott that really matter, I see a much greater range of quality within that list than is usually allowed. They all contain splendid things, representing Scott at his best. But three stand out from the others for the range of their interests, the sustained merit of their writing, and the superior impact of their total effect; and they are, in order of composition, *Waverley*, *Rob Roy*, and the *Heart of Midlothian*. Since these three are also the novels of Scott closest to the epic kind, I shall not, in explaining their merits, be straying from my chosen theme.

In selecting these three I do not deny that the other Scottish novels list include the greater themes with which they have been credited. Morton in *Old Mortality* is indeed a symbol of reconciliation: a high-minded moderate who is critical of both Covenanters and high Tories. The *Bride of Lammermoor* presents the tragic consequences when the old and the new ways of life are insisted on in extreme forms and admit of no reconciliation. The great themes run through the whole series, but only in the three I have named do they thoroughly permeate their contexts.

Writers on Scott have not always made it clear that he pursued his great themes in ethics as well as in politics. The root-principle of all his three masterpieces of fiction is the need to reconcile the sanguine element in a person or a people with the conditions of life actually existing at a given time. To whatever nobility the sanguine element could propel a person or a people, it could only lead to disaster if it operated in hostile conditions of life. Scott himself achieved some kind of reconciliation; his heart bled for Byron, who could not—"what a pity that a man of such exquisite genius will not be contented to be happy on the ordinary terms!" The theme is perennial and it was strong in Scott's day. Peacock agreed with Scott and accepted the ordinary terms; he was Shelley's friend and he lamented Shelley's refusal to accept them, as Scott lamented Byron's. Jane Austen was for reconciling sensibility with sense. Both she and Peacock treated the theme in comic terms. Peacock was political as well as ethical. Scott included ethical and political, comic and tragic. He has far the greatest scope. Just as Byron was a tragic figure, so certain ways of life, especially the old feudal and chivalrous life of the Highlands, became tragic when extended into hostile and irreconcilable conditions. The theme could assume epic proportions if it were treated with great variety and intensity and if it included convincingly the picture of its two elements reconciled. Conditions in Scotland favoured a convincing picture. The country, divided and obscure at the time of the Union, had brought itself to face the conditions of modern life; it was proud of its intellectual and industrial achievements; and it wished to reconcile the parts of itself that had been in conflict. It was ready to use the right mouthpiece for its wishes; and in a way that for England had become impossible for almost a hundred years. Up to a point Scott was the right mouthpiece.

I shall now go on to comment on the three novels that constitute Scott's main title to be a writer of epic. On *Waverley* I shall have most to say, not because it is better than the other two but because it offers a good opportunity for making observations that hold good for all the best of Scott, for instance that on the intensity of some of his writing.

(v) *'Waverley'*

(a) *Traditional Character*

Among the three novels under review, *Waverley* has the greatest wealth of inherited themes and styles. Also, it is intense in parts; it contains memorable major characters; it is beautifully, if rather too abundantly, plotted; and generally it is the most diversified of all Scott's novels. It also presents quite clearly the great theme of reconciliation: both of nation with nation and of the romantic with the rational temper in the individual. Yet, unlike *Rob Roy* and the *Heart of Midlothian*, it presents the theme rather than develops it powerfully. Thus, it cannot stand as an achieved epic in its own right, however eminent its contribution to Scott's epic area. I will deal with the topics I have just indicated, in order; and I begin with that of inherited themes and styles.

More openly as well as more truly than the other novels *Waverley* draws sustenance from the eighteenth century. In his first chapter Scott tells us that the story will essentially be of men not of manners, that his concern is with the passions, due allowance being made for the forms these assumed at different periods:

> It is from the great book of Nature, the same through a thousand editions, whether of black-letter or wire-wove and hot-pressed, that I have venturously essayed to read a chapter to the public.

Fielding made the same claim for *Tom Jones*; and if *Waverley* approaches the epic it is largely by way of the great eighteenth-century mode of comic fiction. The tone is genial and kindly enough, but consistently spiced with a grain or two of satire. I have already compared the style of one passage with Congreve's. It is not unique, witness this second passage. The scene is the tea-table of an Edinburgh house during the slack period between the Battle of Prestonpans and the march south. Waverley has read scenes from *Romeo and Juliet* and Flora has given her opinion that Romeo's transference of affection from Rosalind to Juliet is not against nature.

76

"Good now, Miss Mac-Ivor," said a young lady of quality, "do you mean to cheat us out of our prerogative? will you persuade us love cannot subsist without hope, or that the lover must become fickle if the lady is cruel? O fie! I did not expect such an unsentimental conclusion."

"A lover, my dear Lady Betty, may, I conceive, persevere in his suit under very discouraging circumstances. Affection can (now and then) withstand very severe storms of rigour, but not a long polar frost of downright indifference. Don't, even with *your* attractions, try the experiment upon any lover whose faith you value. Love will subsist on wonderfully little hope, but not altogether without it."

But Scott makes it plain that he is being very much himself when he adds:

"It will be just like Duncan Mac-Girdie's mare," said Evan, "if your ladyships please; he wanted to use her by degrees to live without meat, and just as he had put her on a straw a day, the poor thing died!"

Scott's gently satirical comedy reaches its height in the incident of the Baron of Bradwardine exercising his feudal right of pulling off the Prince Regent's boots. That incident is in the pure tradition of eighteenth-century comedy; just as the great figure of the Baron himself is, with his innocence, his absurdity, and his nobility, kin to Parson Adams.

It is, however, the hero who touches the eighteenth century at most points. I am puzzled that Grierson should approximate Waverley to Don Quixote on account of their common proneness to romantic imaginings, for Scott carefully warns us against such an approximation at the beginning of the fifth chapter. But if Waverley barely touches Don Quixote, he unites in himself two later types much used in the eighteenth century: the innocent young hero who learns much by experience, Gil Blas and Candide, and the alien visitor who, seeing the country he visits with new eyes, gives a truer account of it than a native, familiar with his surroundings, could attain to. Waverley, Scott's one hero with a fully developing character, lives more vividly than the innocents from whom he derives. And as the Citizen of the World he expresses more than his forebears because he represents some of the features of his own country as well as reveals those of the country he visits. He is, in fact, the main agent of that mode of reconciliation which, as I have said, Scott's epic area above all concerns. But the development of Waverley's character and his function as reconciler are topics that must be held over. My present point is that *Waverley* gains a kind of stability and repose unique among the Scottish novels, in being so solidly in the line of the eighteenth century. One may guess further that it did so because it is Scott's earliest novel, begun nine years before publication; and early work is usually more traditional than later. Conceived in greater leisure than the other novels, no wonder if *Waverley* has a greater air of repose.

(b) *Intensity*

As well as being the most reposeful, the novel which perhaps requires the slowest reading, *Waverley* along with *Rob Roy* and the *Heart of Midlothian* is the most intensely written. It is not exempt from passages where the style is drearily pompous and long-winded in the worst post-Johnsonian manner. But that is an ill to which all Scott's novels are prone, and which, being occasional and inorganic, we are justified in passing over lightly. Such passages excepted, the writing of *Waverley* either has the ease of motion that comes from an intense focusing of the mind on the object or quickens through an intensity of passion. The opening chapters, describing Waverley's circumstances and how he came to visit Scotland, have been called tedious and spun out. I can only admire the serene confidence with which Scott manipulates his setting. He has decided the exact extent of staging, or weight of fact required, to convince us that Waverley's visit was probable. I no more doubt these circumstances than I doubt the solidity of the monastery described at the beginning of the *Brothers Karamazov*. The same confidence, accompanied by a quickening of feeling, extends to the account of the village and castle of Tully-Veolan. There is much description in Scott, and as he went on writing he was apt to describe the same kind of scene, particularly the area of Scotland where Highlands and Lowlands meet. Through this very abundance one tends to read description more slackly than dialogue. Yet nowhere better than in the

SCOTT

descriptions can one detect Scott's quality, his range from the intense to the merely competent. In the village and castle of Tully-Veolan every detail stands out separate and memorable, and we follow Waverley as he makes his way through them. In contrast, Argyle's castle at Inverary as described in the *Legend of Montrose* leaves a vague, romantic, Gothic blur on the mind. Scott maintains the intensity of his descriptive power throughout *Waverley*. Tully-Veolan after the soldiers have defaced it is as memorable as when first described. Witness, for instance, the following detail:

> In one compartment of this old-fashioned garden were two immense horse-chestnut trees, of whose size the Baron was particularly vain: too lazy, perhaps, to cut them down, the spoilers, with malevolent ingenuity, had mined them, and placed a quantity of gunpowder in the cavity. One had been shivered to pieces by the explosion, and the wreck lay scattered around, encumbering the ground it had so long shadowed. The other mine had been more partial in its effect. About one-fourth of the trunk of the tree was torn from the mass, which, mutilated and defaced on one side, still spread on the other its ample and undiminished boughs.

It is not only in the descriptions of nature that Scott displays the intensity of his apprehension through the memorable details; he succeeds equally in his scenes of action. Thus in describing the preliminaries of the Battle of Prestonpans he is aware not only of the armies but of the spectators:

> From the neighbouring hamlets, the peasantry cautiously shewed themselves, as if watching the issue of the expected engagement; and at no great distance in the bay were two square-rigged vessels, bearing the English flag, whose tops and yards were crowded with less timid spectators.

The sailors in the rigging have no bearing on the battle itself but a most definite bearing on the intensity with which we are made to see it.

(c) *Point of View*

One means of intensity, absent elsewhere in Scott, is his use of his hero in fixing the point of view. Only in *Waverley* does

Scott both intend to present events through the eyes of his hero and succeed in this intention. I do not mean that in *Waverley* Scott never altered his point of vision or that he looked through the eyes of his hero as faithfully as Defoe did through those of the narrator of the *Journal of the Plague Year*. But, in common with most novels that are supposed to present one angle of vision, *Waverley* gets its main effects filtered through the glasses of a single man. Such general fidelity serves to make any departures from it the more prominent. There are several of these (apart from the scenes from which Waverley is absent and hence where his vision would be irrelevant), and their existence should be recorded, since through them Scott exhibits a refinement of technique he is not always thought capable of. For instance, in the thirteenth chapter Waverley, the Baron, and the Rev. Mr Rubrick adjourn to Rose Bradwardine's sitting-room to drink coffee. She sings them a ballad and mentions a sequel to the story it tells. The Baron, who knows the sequel, remarks that it is a figment of a superstitious age. Whereupon,

> "My father has a strange defiance of the marvellous, Captain Waverley," observed Rose, "and once stood firm when a whole synod of presbyterian divines were put to the rout by a sudden apparition of the foul fiend."
> Waverley looked as if desirous to hear more.
> "Must I tell my story as well as sing my song?—Well—Once upon a time . . ."

The point of view changes when Waverley makes no answer to the speech Rose addresses to him but merely looks desirous. His external appearance is substituted for his subjective comment on the scene. How Waverley appears to Rose and what she thinks about him supplants what Waverley thinks about her and her setting. And, when she asks her rhetorical question, we see her doing her little best to tell her story well and to get all the response she can from the handsome English stranger who has appeared so unexpectedly at the castle. Scott restores the normal line of vision as soon as Rose has told her tale.

(d) *Intensity Again*

Scott, therefore, is no slave to the concentrated vision. But he mainly employs it and achieves thereby the intensity which is its proper aim. Now this intensity is so different from what usually passes as Scott's characteristic virtue, namely an abundant and sprawling energy, capable of overwhelming you if you do not keep too tight a hold on your critical sense, and is so crucial to the epic effect, that I must give some space to arguing that in *Waverley* it is really there.

I take as my illustrations the Battle of Prestonpans and the preliminaries, in Carlisle Castle, to the execution of Fergus.

I have never heard it actually said and yet I believe this to be true: that two generations who have known war from experience suspect Scott of having abused the topic. Even if you make every allowance for the nature of war having changed, this suspicion is not unmerited. When Scott's imagination is least engaged, when he is being merely fluent for the public amusement, he can treat war and scenes of violence with offensive cheerfulness or indifference. In fact, he is guilty of a kind of inverted sentimentalism, the sentimentalism of callousness and superficiality. For this he has indeed the excuse of being naturally pugnacious. I do not mean he was quarrelsome, but he had just that warmth of mind that yields readily to the single-minded and blinkered excitement of old-fashioned warfare, as well as to the glamour of daring and desperate causes. He was well aware of this side of his nature. He wrote to Miss Clapham at the time he was busy with *Waverley*:

> Seriously I am very glad I did not live in 1745 for though as a lawyer I could not have pleaded Charles's right and as a clergyman I could not have prayed for him yet as a soldier I would I am sure against the convictions of my better reason have fought for him even to the bottom of the gallows.[1]

But Scott's excuse reaches only part way, for he was guilty at times of exhibiting in a pretty cool mood a kind of simple and primitive exaltation which can flourish genuinely and legitimately only at the highest temperatures. Nor can you claim

---

[1] *Letters 1811-14, ed. cit.*, p. 302.

that Scott treated war so conventionally that in his pages you need not take it seriously. Dumas may escape happily on such a plea. But Scott *could* exercise the most lively and delicate imagination in treating it. Such an exercise makes it the more deplorable that he should have abused the topic in other places; but there it is and it must in justice be recognised apart from the abuse. Once again we must be prepared for anything.

Read without prejudice, the tale of the battle at Prestonpans completely evades the suspicion that Scott abused the art of war and, presented through the eyes of Waverley, it achieves the greatest intensity. When Scott is forced, for the sake of completing his story, to generalise, he is short, businesslike, and unsentimental. To illustrate the intensity, take first a few sentences from the account of the two sides approaching on the day before the actual field. Fergus's troop, to which Waverley was attached, were holding a point of vantage; and the account proceeds:

> To check or dislodge this party, the English general detached two guns, escorted by a strong party of cavalry. They approached so near that Waverley could plainly recognize the standard of the troop he had formerly commanded, and hear the trumpets and kettle-drums sound the advance, which he had so often obeyed. He could hear, too, the well-known word given in the English dialect, by the equally well-distinguished voice of the command-ing officer, for whom he had felt so much respect. It was at that instant that, looking around him, he saw the wild dress and appearance of his Highland associates, heard their whispers in an uncouth and unknown language, looked upon his own dress, so unlike that which he had worn from his infancy, and wished to awake from what seemed at the moment a dream, strange, horrible, and unnatural.

To comment on a single detail, the general difference of the opposing sides, symbolised by the commands given in clear English and by the Gaelic mutterings of the Highlanders, owes its vividness to Waverley's personal and specialised knowledge of both sounds.

When Scott comes to describe the first encounter, he does so through the eyes of Waverley. The things that occur are all strictly within his personal ken and they are authentic, revealing and not sentimentalising the nature of one kind of war. Fergus and his Highlanders are as convincing as Homer's warriors in ambush trembling with excitement:

"Down with your plaid, Waverley," cried Fergus, throwing off his own; "we'll win silks for our tartans before the sun is above the sea."

The clansmen on every side stript their plaids, prepared their arms, and there was an awful pause of about three minutes, during which the men, pulling off their bonnets, raised their faces to heaven, and uttered a short prayer. Waverley felt his heart at that moment throb as it would have burst from his bosom. It was not fear, it was not ardour,—it was a compound of both, a new and deeply energetic impulse, that with its first emotion chilled and astounded, then fevered and maddened his mind. The sounds around him combined to exalt his enthusiasm; the pipes played, and the clans rushed forward, each in its own dark column. As they advanced they mended their pace, and the muttering sounds of the men to each other began to swell into a wild cry.

At this moment, the sun, which was now above the horizon, dispelled the mist. The vapours rose like a curtain, and showed the two armies in the act of closing. The line of the regulars was formed directly fronting the attacks of the Highlanders; it glittered with the appointments of a complete army, and was flanked by cavalry and artillery. But the sight impressed no terror on the assailants.

"Forward, sons of Ivor," cried their Chief, "or the Camerons will draw the first blood!"

They rushed on with a tremendous yell.

It indicates the command Scott had of all his faculties that after this short and thrilling passage he can coolly go on to remark, "The rest is well known."

The scene of Fergus's execution, described with great economy, gains in richness through the unexpected way in which it develops Fergus's already convincing character. Freed from the distractions of political intrigue and contemptuous of the barbarities of cutting down and disembowelling which, as convicted of high treason, he is about to suffer, he is delicately considerate of his friend's tender heart and will not allow him to witness the actual execution. In their last meeting in the

courtyard of Carlisle Castle Waverley offers to follow him to
the place of execution without.

"We part not *here!*" said Waverley.

"O yes, we do; you must come no farther. Not that I fear what
is to follow for myself. Nature has her tortures as well as art; and
how happy should we think the man who escapes from the
throes of a mortal and painful disorder, in the space of a short
half hour! And this matter, spin it out as they will, cannot last
longer. But what a dying man can suffer firmly, may kill a living
friend to look upon.—This same law of high treason," he continued with astonishing firmness and composure, "is one of the
blessings, Edward, with which your free country has accom-
modated poor old Scotland—her own jurisprudence, as I have
heard, was much milder."

I find Fergus's measured rhetoric, so consistent with his
aristocratic French upbringing and the doctrine of *sprezzatura*
that ruled all the aristocracies in the tradition of the Renaissance, a great deal more convincing than that of Meg
Merrilies. Further, Fergus's sophistication even at this terrible
moment serves to set off the simpler grief and horror of the
younger, less experienced, and kindlier man. This is the final
paragraph of the scene in Carlisle Castle:

The last of the soldiers had now disappeared from under the
vaulted arch-way through which they had been filing for several
minutes; the court-yard was now totally empty, but Waverley
still stood there as if stupified, his eyes fixed upon the dark pass
where he had so lately seen the last glimpse of his friend. At
length, a female servant of the governor, struck with compassion
at the stupified misery which his countenance expressed, asked
him, if he would not walk into her master's house and sit down?
She was obliged to repeat her question twice ere he compre-
hended her, but at length it recalled him to himself. Declining
the courtesy by a hasty gesture, he pulled his hat over his eyes,
and, leaving the Castle, walked as swiftly as he could through
the empty streets, till he regained his inn, then threw himself
into an apartment, and bolted the door.

In about an hour and a half, which seemed an age of unutter-
able suspense, the sound of the drums and fifes, performing a
lively air, and the confused murmur of the crowd which now
filled the streets, so lately deserted, apprized him that all was

finished, and that the military and populace were returning from the dreadful scene. I will not attempt to describe his sensations.

What most gives the passage its grip and its sting is the unexpected intervention of the 'female servant'. This is one of those strokes which, evidently unpremeditated, betoken the creative imagination working at its height. We are looking through Waverley's eyes at the now empty arch and experience an amalgam of feeling composed of thoughts about Fergus's fate and thoughts about its effect on the mind of Waverley. The intervention of the servant jerks us out of his mind to a point in the deserted courtyard where we can watch the outward signs of his misery. And it is highly suggestive as well as surprising. We are not told the details of Waverley's thoughts, but from our now long familiarity with his vivid imagination, his capacity for reflection, and his most humane temperament, we can be certain they included a deep horror of what man could make of man, and the intense loneliness of being individually horrified at what for the mass was a welcome holiday excitement. Stupefied by such thoughts, he is the victim of a cruel irony: for he cannot perceive, as the reader immediately does, that the small, pure act of kindness on the part of the servant represents the other, compensating, part of the human paradox; just as Adam and Eve in *Paradise Lost* fail to see that the first feeble motions of their minds towards reconciliation after their quarrel are destined to compensate for all the fury of evil that their initial sin has let loose.

I have spent so long on the scenes in Carlisle Castle—and I believe them the equal of any scenes in English fiction—because they show so plainly qualities which Scott is usually denied. It was a pity that he did not draw more often (as here he did) on the deepest places in his mind and that he was so suspicious of its secret life; but he visited its depths often enough to rank with the greatest. These matters refer to Scott generally. My immediate concern is with *Waverley*, and my immediate point is that if such great scenes can grow naturally out of their context (as I find that they do) and are not mere isolated and exceptional splendours, they argue a high eminence that is one of the epic's prerequisites.

(e) *The Characters*

A common criticism of *Waverley* is that it is immature as lacking the wealth of comic characters which constitutes Scott's highest accomplishment. The truth is that *Waverley* is not immature but exceptional: it is the novel in which the major characters count for most. I have already asserted that its hero is unique among Scott's heroes in the fullness with which his character is developed. The same fullness applies to the three other main characters, Fergus and Flora Mac-Ivor and the Baron of Bradwardine. The two Mac-Ivors, of the most aristocratic Highland stock and French on their mother's side, brought up in the sophistication of the Stuart court in its French exile, Catholic in religion, and dedicated to the Jacobite cause, are cunningly set apart and diversified from all the others. Fergus is quite at home in his part of Highland chieftain, Flora takes a sincere antiquarian interest in Highland folk-lore; but they are not identified with the land of Britain. They remain slightly alien, more Continental than British, coolly sure of their manners in a way more French than Scottish, and, under their polish, extreme. They help incalculably to promote that acute awareness of national differences which distinguishes *Waverley*. For all their likeness, however, they are clearly differentiated. Fergus is the politician with an eye to swift action, not too scrupulous in getting what he wants and too sanguine over getting it because he wants it so much. Flora is the idealist, and her Jacobitism differs from her brother's: "her loyalty as it exceeded her brother's in fanaticism, excelled it also in purity". These differences come into the open when Flora refuses Waverley's offer of marriage. Bred in France, accepting the doctrine of the marriage of convenience, and carried away by the political advantages of the match, Fergus simply cannot understand Flora's reluctance. Nor is it surprising, for Flora does not disapprove of all marriages of convenience. But she has a finer mind than her brother and scruples that make it impossible for her to consent to the match however advantageous. Waverley, to her thinking, falls short of what she demands of a love-match and is of too fine a sensibility to be sacrificed to one of convenience. He

could never be a hero like his ancestor Sir Nigel, and such a
here is the only man Flora can love; but by a lower standard
he is much to be esteemed and he must be rewarded with a
bride who can sincerely love him. She tells Waverley that if he
had been a less sensitive type of man he would have had a
better chance of winning her as a dutiful and unaffectionate
mate. Her insight into Waverley's character is terribly accurate; and she judges him generally on the two standards by
which she settled his proposal of marriage. By her own fanatical
standards he is contemptible: by the standards of ordinary
human requirements he is sensitive, amiable, generous, even
brave; and, recognising the claims of those standards though
they are not hers, she does what she can to help him. Scott
reveals the characters of the Mac-Ivors gradually and causes
them to change during the course of the book. At the very
end both act in ways that surprise us but which convince us at
the same time. I have already noted the unexpected delicacy
of Fergus's behaviour to Waverley, when politics are irrelevant
and he is about to die a barbarous death. But what served to
confirm Fergus's character ended in nearly breaking Flora's.
To be consistent with her heroic ideal she should have exulted
in her brother's martyrdom. But, instead, she blames herself,
not for their common fidelity to the Jacobite cause and her
part in strengthening him in it, but for allowing her fanaticism
to impair her judgement, which ought to have told her that the
rebellion could only issue in disaster. She ends full of remorse
that she did not dissuade her brother from an impossibility.

The Baron of Bradwardine is a simple-minded man but not
a simple character. Compare him with Scott's other version
of the soldier-pedant, Dugald Dalgetty in *Montrose*, and the
differences show up. We know Dugald's formula very quickly,
and it remains unaltered throughout the book. Quite rightly,
for a developing character would be out of place in a book on
which the Novel of Terror has left a considerable mark. What
complicates the Baron so agreeably is the unworldliness and
essential humility that goes with his pedantry. And it is only
step by step that we become aware of the extent of those
qualities. His duel with the Laird of Balmawhapple for having
insulted Waverley, then his guest, both surprises us and reveals

his character. But more surprising still (when we reflect on the whole incident) is his utter absence of pride in having chastised a younger and, one would have assumed, more active man than himself. His motive was simple obedience to a code he accepted without question. He is unworldly in money matters and gets no share of the Chevalier's funds for the maintenance of his army. Naturally, he is unconscious of ridicule. But the Baron's character is not fully developed till the very end, when he is in hiding from the English soldiery. Here he endures his discomforts with a serenity and an absence of complaint which at once surprise and convince. The situation is not just something he repeats but something he has grown into.

Waverley's character changes most of all. Not only is he the innocent let loose in the world and the alien using his eyes, but the young man who grows up. He is the young romantic, slightly ridiculous as well as generous, who gradually sheds his illusions through the discipline of crude and genuine experience. As the potential lover he is the young man "looking out for some object whose affection may dignify him in his own eyes". And this is his state of mind near the beginning of his Highland expedition, undertaken as no more than a romantic holiday:

> He had now time to give himself up to the full romance of his situation. Here he sate on the banks of an unknown lake, under the guidance of a wild native, whose language was unknown to him, on a visit to the den of some renowned outlaw, a second Robin Hood perhaps, or Adam o' Gordon, and that at deep midnight, through scenes of difficulty and toil, separated from his attendant, left by his guide:—What a fund of circumstances for the exercise of a romantic imagination, and all enhanced by the solemn feeling of uncertainty at least, if not of danger! The only circumstance which assorted ill with the rest was the cause of his journey—the Baron's milk cows! this degrading incident he kept in the background.

It was not only the theft of the Baron's cattle that he kept in the background but the welfare of the men he had brought from England to serve with him in his cavalry regiment. How were *they* faring during his prolonged furlough? Very ill, as he learnt later to his distress, from the mouth of one of them, his late sergeant, now a captive and on the point of death. He beholds "with sincere sorrow, and no slight tinge of remorse, the final agonies of mortality, now seen for the first time". *Now seen for the first time*: the sight is part of the process of Waverley's education. And as he moves away with the Pretender's army towards Prestonpans, "the repeated expostulation of Houghton—'Ah, squire, why did you leave us?' rung like a knell in his ears". And he reflects bitterly on the consequences of an indolent and undecided mind. The moral 'only connect', which E. M. Forster set at the head of one of his novels, applies to Waverley's conduct, as well as to other things in Scott's first novel. Waverley succeeds in growing up, and without losing his humanity and generosity. He will not be bullied by Fergus and he learns to act promptly and responsibly. Scott may be a little too explicit for some tastes about a process which had become clear enough through the testimony of events. Waverley, the Jacobite cause lost, is living *incognito* in the Lake District:

> It was in many a winter walk by the shores of Ulswater, that he acquired a more complete mastery of a spirit tamed by adversity than his former experience had given him; and that he felt himself entitled to say firmly, though perhaps with a sigh, that the romance of his life was ended, and that its real history had now commenced.

Whether or not Scott is being too explicit here, his account of Waverley's appearance, when at long last he returns to Waverley-Honour, successfully implies the same process:

> The appearance of Waverley, embrowned by exercise, and dignified by the habits of military discipline, had acquired an athletic and hardy character, which not only verified the Colonel's narrative, but surprised and delighted all the inhabitants of Waverley-Honour.

And Scott returns beautifully to the ironic tone of the novel's opening when his uncle the Baronet and his aunt hear Colonel Talbot's account of Waverley's share in the Battle of Prestonpans:

> The imagination of the Baronet and his sister ranked the exploits of Edward with those of Wilibert, Hildebrand, and Nigel, the vaunted heroes of their line.

And we remember Flora's cool appraisal of Waverley and her assertion that heroism such as Sir Nigel's was quite beyond his scope.

The theme of Waverley's education touches the novel's plot as well as the hero's character and is one of the things that provide coherence. And beautifully coherent the plot is. By modern tastes there is too much of it, or rather too great a wealth of detail. The comedy of Waverley's journey to London with Mrs Nosebag could be spared and some of the machinations of Donald Bean Lean. But the main lines of the action are beautifully disposed, and the timing of its main changes is perfect. For instance, at precisely the moment when we have had our fill, and not a scrap more than our fill, of Tully-Veolan Scott recalls our attention to Waverley's military position and then, in a new chapter, introduces the new theme of the Highlands. I attribute this perfection in timing partly to the length of years Scott had to meditate on his theme; a remark that leads to the topic of the conscious will and hence to that of epic fulfilment.

(f) *Epic Quality*

If Scott was lacking in any quality that creates the epic, it was in that of the prolonged exercise of the conscious will. He composed at high pressure and great speed and, generally speaking, he improvised more and reflected less, progressively during his career as a novelist. It never occurred to him to put all he was good for into a single great work. It is, however, possible for a man to achieve something resembling the prolonged exercise of the conscious will if he can use the accumulated products of past reflection as fuel for the fires of intensive creation. This is a different process from reflecting and creating simultaneously, which is the true epic process, that of Dante and Milton. But it can at least contribute to an epic effect. In all three of Scott's novels which I think the greatest this process occurs. He draws on his accumulated reflections on life in general and on the politics of Scotland and England in particular. But in *Waverley*, as not in the other two, he developed, and not merely drew on, his previously accumulated reflections, during composition. Thus, as a pondered work of art, *Waverley* is the best thing he did. And it is the best in this way because it was the first and, as such, was free from the hurry to satisfy a hungry public.

On the other hand it is less successful than *Rob Roy* and the *Heart of Midlothian* in finding fitting expression for the great national and political themes. It has a splendid range through comedy, kindly irony, tragedy, sound and subtle psychology: abundant material for the successful issue from it of a choric effect. But that effect can find no worthy vehicle. Scott is indeed concerned with what can be vaguely called the soul of Scotland, and that soul in his own day. And he presents noble things in a Scotland of sixty years ago that may even then have been an anachronism but which ought to be preserved in some different way: the devotion of the Mac-Ivors to a doomed cause, the feudal loyalty of Evan Maccombich, the religious simplicity of the Baron's pedantry. Scott is equally aware of evil or cruel things which he would like to see purged from the soul of Scotland. The Highlanders respect Waverley's concern for his dying retainer, but only because the man was his retainer:

> They would not have understood the general philanthropy, which rendered it almost impossible for Waverley to have past any person in such distress; but, as apprehending that the sufferer was one of his *following*, they unanimously allowed that Waverley's conduct was that of a kind and considerate chieftain, who merited the attachment of his people.

The Highlanders are deficient in general humanity and Waverley can teach them a lesson. On the other side Colonel Talbot is a fine specimen of an Englishman, but he is intolerant of the Highlanders, and here Waverley can teach him a lesson. In fact, what I believe Scott had in mind was that the true soul of Scotland should be compounded of the loyalties and heroisms of the country's past, softened and humanised by the greater tolerance of England at its best. Fergus's dying request to Waverley is that he will relieve the folk of his clan in the distress they are likely to suffer in the aftermath of the rebellion. Waverley pledged his word and redeemed his pledge, and "his memory still lives in these glens by the name of Friend of the Sons of Ivor". And this is only one of many expressions of the theme of Scottish loyalty and English humanity. The trouble is that Waverley, wonderfully successful in his treble part of innocent in the world, open-eyed alien, and young romantic educated by experience, cannot support this additional duty: he simply lacks the weight and the stamina required. And he is almost alone in this his fourth function. True, there is the "good Mr Morton", the peace-making pastor of the parish of Cairnvreckan, who befriended Waverley when under arrest; but he appears in this episode alone and is not powerfully enough drawn to make himself felt outside it. And, generally, Scott never leaves us in doubt of his own belief in the sympathetic imagination and in reconciliation. But, however many are the references to this master-theme, there is nothing, either episode or person, capable of pulling them together and giving them strength and intensity. I do not mean that the novel fails in consequence. I merely mean that on the epic side it does not quite make good and that the epic effect, which I believe Scott intended, fails to match the novel's conspicuous success in other ways.

Nevertheless, as exhibiting the data of a choric effect, as exposing the problems of Highland and Lowland, England and Scotland, *Waverley* is highly important in the epic area which I believe the best of Scott's novels to compose.

(vi) Between 'Waverley' and 'Rob Roy'

(a) 'Guy Mannering' and 'The Antiquary'

Guy Mannering and the *Antiquary* succeeded *Waverley*; and Scott tells us in the preface to the *Antiquary* that the three novels illustrate the manners of three different ages of Scotland beginning with the year 1745 and approaching his own by intervals of, roughly, twenty-five years. He adds that in the last two he expends his energies largely on the less polished types of mankind on the Wordsworthian plea that in these the passions have freer vent and receive more eloquent expression. And he adds:

> I have been more solicitous to describe manners minutely, than to arrange in any case an artificial and combined narration, and have but to regret that I felt myself unable to unite these two requisites of a good Novel.

If Scott is here thinking more of *Guy Mannering* and the *Antiquary* than of *Waverley* he is being a good self-critic, for the virtues of these two novels lie in their wonderful repertory of comic characters and in their scenes of domestic life. He tried to organise these scenes by the old and much-used theme of the long-lost heir and to render them more palatable by exciting and improbable episodes. Scott, with his exuberant invention, had not the least difficulty in fabricating these; and in a letter (not in the preface) he reveals his motive for doing so. Writing on 16th May 1816[1] he declared that the *Antiquary* was less interesting than *Guy Mannering* because "the period did not admit of so much romantic situation". This is an interesting remark because it shows us Scott's sense of duty as he conceived it, his duty to entertain his public by 'romantic situation' rather than to please himself. It shows us why he decided to attach his enchanting pictures of Scottish manners to the stale romance of the missing heir and why he must interpolate early into the *Antiquary* the exciting but inept scene of Sir Arthur and Isabella Wardour together with Lovel cut off by the tide, joined by Edie Ochiltree, and nearly losing their lives. He thought he owed such inept excitement to his public. The two books are so good in parts that they will continue to attract readers, but it is vain to pretend that either succeeds as a whole.

Nevertheless, both add something to the extent and the nature of Scott's epic area. I cannot follow Daiches[2] in thinking seriously of Sir Arthur Wardour as representing the decadence and present ineptitude of the stiffer and stupider type of Scottish Tory aristocrat: the trend of the book does not persuade me to look on him in that light. I cannot extract more than a comic significance from him. Nor should I be willing to justify the scene of high-tide peril which brings Oldbuck and Sir Arthur together again after their quarrel as a symbol of how Whigs and Tories in modern Scotland ought to remember they are all good Scotsmen and to forget their

---

[1] *Letters 1815-17*, p. 233.

[2] David Daiches's important criticism of Scott is to be found in *Nineteenth Century Fiction* for 1951 and in his introduction to the *Heart of Midlothian* (New York 1948).

differences when the good of their country demands it. Or, to turn to *Guy Mannering*, the Englishness of the title character cannot compare in significance with the Englishness of Waverley. Thus, I cannot bring myself to believe that these two novels enlarge Scott's epic area considerably. But the gipsies in *Guy Mannering* and Edie Ochiltree in the *Antiquary* add something to the political data or revelations given in *Waverley*. The gipsies on the Ellangowan estate had been settled and tolerated there for many years. They had grown into their setting, and though they might commit a petty offence or two they were loyal to their landlord and abided by certain traditional rules. They considered themselves part of the social organism. Bertram in turning them out may have had the technicality of the law on his side, but he offended against something more important, a human adjustment made sacred by the test of time. Edie Ochiltree, again, though a beggar, was an organic part of the social body and was proud of his profession. He thought he gave good value in return for the alms he received, and Scott agrees that he did. Averse to a steady occupation in a single place, he fulfils in his vagrancy a function that no peasant or mechanic could fulfil. Through the gipsies and Edie and their proved place in society Scott expressed obliquely what Burke expressed by explicit oratory, his belief in the sanctity of the adjustments that have been made over the years by the human process of trial and error. Scott ridiculed the political and social habits that had outlived their use and failed to work, but if a habit did actually work he could not bear to see it slighted and destroyed on an abstract principle. If Scotland was to keep or re-create its soul, it must hold fast to whatever in its institutions was genuinely alive. This faith does not appear in *Waverley* and it is what his next two novels contributed to the epic task Scott was unconsciously attempting.

(b) *'Old Mortality'*

In what I have to say about *Old Mortality* I find myself obliged to go against the opinions of the best judges. Scott himself "preferred it to any fictitious narrative I have been able to produce". Later critics, recognising the seriousness of many of the characters, the brilliance and the thoroughness of the historical reconstruction, and the clarity of its political moralising, have habitually classed it among the three or four masterpieces of Scott, inferior in pathos to the *Heart of Midlothian* perhaps but the sternest and the grandest of them all. There are signs too that Scott took *Old Mortality* more seriously than his other novels. He wrote:

> There are noble subjects for narrative during that period full of the strongest light and shadow, all human passions stirr'd up and stimulated by the most powerful motives, and the contending parties as distinctly contrasted in manners and in modes of thinking as in political principles. I am complete master of the whole history of these strange times both of persecutors and persecuted so I trust I have come decently off.[1]

Scott may even have had a conscious eye to an epic effect. There are among the chief characters a noble hero, his chivalrous opponent, and a great commander. There are prophecies in the high epic manner: Mucklewrath at the point of death foretells the fall of the Stuarts; Claverhouse in his great speech on fame to Morton foretells his own death-in-victory. If any novel of Scott *should* be epic it is *Old Mortality*.

It is easy to see the high political moral, entirely applicable to Scott's own day, that *Old Mortality* ought to present. The conflicting parties, persecutors and persecuted, are presented with the clearest emphasis. Claverhouse is the extreme of Tory aristocracy, polished and nonchalant on the surface, but ruthless towards his enemies and contemptuous of the common man. Balfour of Burley is the uncompromising fanatic on the other side, powerful and cunning in action, but as ready to persecute if he had the chance as are those who hunt him out. Both characters are meant to be grand in their courage and vitality. But they are already anachronisms, survivors into an age which demands something less unyielding and destructive. Each character has his supporters. Then there are the temporisers: Cuddie Headrigg, afflicted with a fanatical mother and unable to temporise as he would like, and the Rev. Peter Poundtext, who keeps his cure of souls under the government

---

[1] *Letters 1815-17*, p. 293.

and evades trouble for as long as he can. But temporising and enlightened toleration are not the same things; and the hero, Morton, is made to stand for the better quality:

> He had inherited from his father an undaunted courage, and a firm and uncompromising detestation of oppression, whether in politics or religion. But his enthusiasm was unsullied by fanatic zeal, and unleavened by the sourness of the puritanical spirit.

Forced into taking sides, he tries to mitigate the violence of his fellows. The dramatic scene near the end where he encounters Burley in hiding, refuses to join him in another desperate attempt at rebellion, and escapes him by jumping a chasm ought to provide the culminating symbol of the new Scotland, dauntless but enlightened, escaping from the useless and out-worn horrors of its fanatical past. On the other side, Lord Evandale, Morton's chivalrous and unsuccessful rival in love, provides a secondary example of courage and enlightened toleration.

In order to fulfil these high aims, *Old Mortality* would have to attain a high degree of coherence. In the mechanics of the plot it does this, but not in the quality of writing, which is subject to large fluctuations. In spite of the plot's imposing façade Scott seems uncertain of himself. He had chosen a period of Scottish history remoter from his own day than any period he had chosen so far; and this may be the reason why the preponderating nature of the novel is that of a carefully prepared historical reconstruction. Such an external conception may suit a certain kind of novel (among Scott's the *Talisman*), but it cannot animate a great political and ethical principle. Nor is it in *Old Mortality* consistent. *Old Mortality* cannot be judged and justified by the criterion of the *Talisman*, because parts of it are far too good. Here are samples of the novel's changing quality. Much of the early part is recounted with ease but little heat; the scene at the inn of Bothwell and Burley wrestling is competent *Talisman* stuff; the feudal dinner at Milnwood, interrupted by Bothwell and his men, is a good interior in the Dutch style; Edith's secret visit to Morton in prison in the Castle of Tullietudlem is told with a depressing mixture of simplicity and archness. The tone may heighten somewhat with the arrival there of Claverhouse and his troop. But in none of these does Scott write at his most intense, from within his subject. A very clear mark of a diminished intensity is that the geography is unemphatic. The landscape does not bite into the mind of the readers. Scott begins to warm up with the preliminaries of the skirmish at Drumclog; but the skirmish itself is not more than a very fine description from without. The attack on the Castle of Tullietudlem is sprightly but somehow frivolous. This is one of the places where Scott abused the theme of war; and the farce of Jenny repelling Cuddie with hot brose, which might have been agreeable enough in another context, is heartless in this one. It is not till Morton is made a prisoner by the Cameronian fanatics and expects to be murdered that Scott fully enters his theme and writes with the intensity he is capable of. From then till Morton is exiled and leaves Scotland Scott writes at his height. Finest of all is the account of the brutal triumph of the victors of Bothwell Brig entering Edinburgh and of stupid and stupefied prisoners. It is intolerably vivid and a terrible indictment of the "fury and the mire of human veins". The presence of such writing reduces the attack on Tullietudlem Castle to frivolity.

What debarred Scott from complete success by any high standard was the perfunctory way he created his hero. Morton has a heavier weight of serious meaning to carry than Waverley, but his creator did not give him a tenth part of the care he gave the other. He is a bore from the very beginning, when he wins the prize at the Wappenshaw, one of the deadly who always get top marks; and his courtship of Edith Bellenden and his rivalry with Lord Evandale with their accompanying misunderstandings and jealousies are stately conventional, most unworthy of the exquisite and living treatment of the love theme in *Waverley*. If Waverley was not quite up to expressing the root-principle of reconciliation which Scott was constantly attempting to formulate, what possible chance had a wooden and yet pretentious character like Morton to do so? No wonder if, debarred from success by the very premises on which he shaped his hero, Scott writes more from his head than from his heart.

In his two next novels Scott tried different methods for

expressing much the same doctrine. In the first of these he relieved the hero of all responsibilities and placed them elsewhere; in the second he substituted for an aristocratic Scotsman a Scottish peasant girl. Both expedients succeeded.

How should we read *Old Mortality* in order to get most out of it? Best, perhaps, as a gallant and elaborate historical reconstruction in the rhetorical style. But we should not, through such a decision, dull our readiness for writing of another kind. When Scott grows intense, we had better enjoy what he gives us, as he gives it, and without lamenting that he cannot write thus all the time.

Read with the other Scottish novels, considered as part of the epic area, *Old Mortality* gains in effect. We can do with the historical reconstructions, with the sweaty efforts to infuriate and enliven Burley and Mucklewrath and to make comic the humbler fanatics, if they are blended with things more truly felt. They enrich the total material of Scotland; they contribute to the epic requirement of amplitude. Like *Guy Mannering* and the *Antiquary*, *Old Mortality* need not be excluded altogether from the epic area.

(vii) *'Rob Roy'*

(a) *Introductory*

There are plenty of faults in *Rob Roy*, but they are all, however large, faults of detail and not of the main substance. Andrew Fairservice as gardener and the same character as gentleman's servant are scarcely the same man. The fight at the inn at Aberfoil is superfluous—there is enough and more important fighting to come—a piece of irrelevant romantic sauce such as Scott thought himself obliged to supply lavishly to please his public. The ending, after Nicol Jarvie has returned to Glasgow and Frank Osbaldistone to Osbaldistone Hall, is very inferior. The novel is by that time virtually over, and Scott did the tidying up with a poor grace. He knew as much, for he wrote:

> I trust you have read Rob by this time. I did not much write him
> *con amore* and I think he smells of the cramp as the Bishop of

Granadas sermon did of the Apoplexy. Above all I had too much flax on my distaff and as it did not consist with my patience or my plan to make a fourth volume I was obliged at last to draw a rough coarse and hasty thread.[1]

It is a very good thing Scott did not spin out the final events into a fourth volume. He would have done well to compress them instead into a crisp summary. As it is, we get a piece of writing like this:

> "Then, traitor, die in your treason!" retorted MacGregor, and plunged his sword in his prostrate antagonist.

There was no need for that sort of stuff to enable Frank to get his Diana and to liquidate the villain, Rashleigh.

Making allowances for these details, I find, contrary to John Buchan, that *Rob Roy* is superbly plotted. But to explain the plot I must first explain the novel's subject-matter. The supposed period of *Rob Roy* is 1715, earlier than that of any previous novel except *Old Mortality*; and yet *Rob Roy* belongs to the Scotland of Scott's day as none of the other novels that constitute Scott's epic area. Scott habitually opposed two ideals or tempers. In *Waverley* the feudalism, the chivalry, and the insubordination of the Highlanders are opposed to English efficiency, before which after a brief success they inevitably go down. In *Guy Mannering* the gipsies' traditional rights conflict with the official and would-be efficient mind. In the *Antiquary* the pride of ancestry of Sir Arthur Wardour is opposed to the Whiggism of Oldbuck. The oppositions in *Old Mortality* have just been mentioned. But none of these oppositions was *especially* apt to Scott's day. In *Rob Roy* Scott took the drastic step of choosing for his opposing pair the new world of commerce and the old world of the clan and the feudal land-owner. Burke in deploring the end of chivalry deplored likewise the apotheosis of the stock-jobber. Scott had the courage to assert that the man of business, the central figure of the new age, must be embodied in the new Scotland. How Scott conveys this I will explain later. For the moment I am concerned with the plot.

[1] *Letters 1817-19*, p. 50.

(b) *The Plot*

The action is divided between England and Scotland, and some critics have thought this division to signify a rift in the structure. In actual fact England and Scotland are closely counterpointed both geographically and through the characters. The scenes in England are either in commercial London or wild Northumberland; those in Scotland are either in commercial Glasgow or the wild Highland valleys of the upper reaches of the Forth. Thus the geographical setting of both countries symbolises the opposition that forms the framework of the novel. The same opposition exists simultaneously in England and Scotland through opposed pairs of characters; but with the difference that the opposition as found in England is more extreme and its ultimate reconciliation less obvious and significant. Sir Hildebrand and especially his sons, living in their ancestral Osbaldistone Hall, represent the last decadence of the feudal, land-owning class. Of the seven sons, the six who relish their country life are boors, and the seventh, who has a brain and wide ambitions, is a villain. William Osbaldistone, Hildebrand's brother and father of the hero, Frank, turned against the feudal life and, migrating to London, pursued a mercantile career with an "ardent spirit of enterprise and speculation". He was a daring type of man who happened to turn his energies to commerce. He becomes stern and uncompromising, and there has been no communication for years between himself and his brother. His son Frank, the hero, is pictured as adventurous but more cultured and flexible than his relations. He is quite successful as the negative hero, as the mere convenience to whom a lot of things happen. We have just sufficient faith in his resolution and decency not to be incredulous when he refuses to go into business and when Diana Vernon finds in him first a relief and a refuge from her boorish cousins and then a resting-place for her love. His only positive duty is faintly to adumbrate the reconciliation of land-owning and commerce. He inherits and occupies Osbaldistone Hall and he is found in the opening chapter, now in his declining years, addressing to William Tresham, the present head of the house of Osbaldistone and Tresham, the memoirs of his youth that compose the novel. The very faintness of his part as reconciler serves to strengthen, by contrast, the prominence of this theme in the Scottish setting.

The opposed characters in Scotland are, simply as characters, more strongly developed than their English counterparts. And, most important, the two dominant characters, one on each side, carry within themselves the healing balm of reconciliation. No third character is needed for the process. The first of the dominant characters is Rob Roy, the Highland outlaw and racketeer, the second is Bailie Nicol Jarvie, the genuine merchant, contrasted among merchants with William Osbaldistone, the successful speculator, and with Messrs MacVittie and MacFin, who are obsequious to the wealthy, and relentless creditors. Both main Scottish characters are men of larger natures than their English counterparts. Rob Roy has his high standards of chivalrous conduct, Nicol Jarvie has a warm and a stout heart. Violently opposed in habits of life and political opinion, they respect each other and allow for what they consider the other's weakness. The kinship in blood is duplicated by a kinship in mind. The matter is summed up in their last parting on the lake shore after the various adventures in the Highlands have reached a satisfactory conclusion:

A boat waited for us in a creek beneath the rock, manned by four lusty Highland rowers; and our host [Rob Roy] took leave of us with great cordiality, and even affection. Betwixt him and Mr Jarvie, indeed, there seemed to exist a degree of mutual regard, which formed a strong contrast to their different occupations and habits. After kissing each other very lovingly, and when they were just in the act of parting, the Bailie, in the fulness of his heart, and with a faultering voice, assured his kinsman, "that if ever an hundred pund, or even twa hundred, would put him or his family in a settled way, he need but just send a line to the Saut-Market"; and Rob, grasping his basket-hilt with one hand, and shaking Mr Jarvie's heartily with the other, protested, "that if ever any body should affront his kinsman, an he would but let him ken, he would stow his lugs out of his head, were he the best man in Glasgow".

By repeating the theme already set forth in England, but with richer circumstance and more emphatically, Scott creates a lovely shape for his novel. Nor does he forget other connections between the two countries. Timber from the oak-forests of the Highlands was the object of some of William Osbaldistone's speculations. Mabel Rickets, Frank's nurse, was an old Northumbrian woman who, living near the Border, had excited Frank's curiosity by many stories of the Scots. If we read the opening chapters of *Rob Roy* with the attention which Scott at his best deserves but rarely receives, we shall find the transition from England to Scotland entirely apt and agreeable.

(c) *Quality of Writing*

As the plot is coherent and the great themes are carried right through, so is the general level of writing very high. The story begins simply with Frank's journey to Northumberland and thickens at an agreeable pace. And, though one may regret a *longueur* here or a paragraph of eighteenth-century pomposity there, Scott is certain of himself as he was not in *Old Mortality*. Fielding could not have bettered the journey north with Frank's feeling of smallness as he is set adrift in the big world, his recovery, and the comedy of his timorous fellow-passenger. Osbaldistone Hall makes a lasting impression on the mind, as the Castle of Tullietudlem failed to do. We retain the picture of its upland situation, its irregular architecture, the sheltered mellowness of the garden within the outer bleakness tended by the Scotch Presbyterian gardener who serves against his humour a Jacobite employer. The masterly Scots dialect of Andrew Fairservice prepares us both for the transfer of the scene to Scotland and for the prolonged and consummate speech of the novel's main character, Bailie Nicol Jarvie. In Glasgow the scenes become massive but they never flag; they are rich in human feelings and in what, if a single word is required, one can only call information, in things we want to know. It is a triumph of art that Scott can animate such massiveness. The urban setting of Glasgow makes as lasting an impression as Osbaldistone Hall. With the transfer of the scene to the valley of the Forth, the scene becomes wild and the action violent. I have called the fight at the inn at Aberfoil superfluous, not because it is not vivid in itself but because there is enough violence without it. And that violence is authentic. It is strange how aptly it follows the massiveness of the scenes in Glasgow. I suppose it is that this massiveness puts the reader's mind in readiness for great things and when great scenes of violence ensue the common grandeur of scale makes the link. Nicol Jarvie, highly comic, is yet one of the most imposing characters in fiction; common in speech, philistine, trade-bound as he is, he has a heroic breadth of heart. It is the awareness of that breadth that makes acceptable the violent scene of the defeat of the British detachment by the High-landers under Rob Roy's wife and her ferocious act of drowning the hostage for Rob Roy's safety. Rob Roy's wife taxes our credulity by talking too long and too rhetorically. But her ferocious act is credible, making true to us the spirit that we apprehend vaguely from the history books when we read of the massacre of Glencoe. In spite of the rhetoric of Rob Roy's wife, Scott generally controls his subject; he is ample enough to convince and swift enough not to tire us; he allows the reader no leisure to doubt; and he ends by elevating what, less intensely conceived, might be a mere succession of exciting events, into the presentation of a whole way of life. And all the time, Nicol Jarvie, Bailie of Glasgow, is present, the unwilling witness and the honest critic of Highland rigour. The pitch is maintained throughout the succeeding scenes of Frank's carrying a message to the British commander who has Rob captive, and of Rob's escape. Great political issues are felt to be involved in thrilling events. It drops a little and becomes more lyrical when Frank, himself a free man again in the confusion, sets out to walk by moonlight along the river bank to the inn of Aberfoil. Lulled and charmed by Scott's lovely descriptive gift, the reader is the more open to the impact of one of the most intense passages Scott attained to: the sudden meeting with Diana and her father, the apparent parting of the lovers for good, Diana's half kiss as she bends to give Frank the packet for which the excursion from Glasgow had been made, and his outburst of uncontrolled emotion. In its intensity it matches the episode of Waverley alone in the courtyard of Carlisle Castle, pitied by the servant girl of the Governor. I give the last paragraphs:

> In the attitude in which she bent from her horse, which was a Highland pony, her face, not perhaps altogether unwillingly,

touched mine—She pressed my hand, while the tear that trembled in her eye found its way to my cheek instead of her own. It was a moment never to be forgotten—inexpressibly bitter, yet mixed with a sensation of pleasure so deeply soothing and affecting, as at once to unlock all the flood-gates of the heart. It was *but* a moment, however; for, instantly recovering from the feeling to which she had involuntarily given way, she intimated to her companion she was ready to attend him, and putting their horses to a brisk pace, they were soon far distant from the place where I stood.

Heaven knows it was not apathy which loaded my frame and my tongue so much, that I could neither return Miss Vernon's half embrace, nor even answer her farewell. The word, though it rose to the tongue, seemed to choke in the throat like the fatal *guilty*, which the delinquent who makes it his plea knows must be followed by the doom of death. The surprise—the sorrow, almost stupified me. I remained motionless with the packet in my hand, gazing after them, as if endeavouring to count the sparkles which flew from the horses' hoofs. I continued to look after even these had ceased to be visible, and to listen for their footsteps long after the distant trampling had died in my ears. At length, tears rushed to my eyes, glazed as they were by the exertion of straining after what was no longer to be seen. I wiped them mechanically, and almost without being aware that they were flowing, but they came thicker and thicker. I felt the tightening of the throat and breast, the *hysterica passio* of poor Lear, and, sitting down by the wayside, I shed a flood of the first and most bitter tears which had flowed from my eyes since childhood.

This is passionate stuff, and those who have been taught that Scott could write but tamely of love will suspect its integrity. But when, in a moment of unusual expansion, he wrote to a correspondent about his feelings for his first love, Williamina Stuart-Belches, he records the same kind of emotional crisis. It is these never-forgotten feelings that animate and intensify Frank's experience. As in the other intense scene in *Waverley*, so here a single incident is the focusing point of the whole passage: Frank gazing after the riders appears "as if endeavouring to count the sparkles which flew from the horses' hoofs". Such observation is usually casual, the fruit of an idle mood. But Frank's passion throws him so utterly off his balance that it bereaves him of all power of action and reduces him to a passive state superficially resembling the idle but actually the remotest possible from it. It is the utter discrepancy between appearance and reality, this total reversal of the normal world, that here moves us so deeply. The mention of Lear in his distress is no anti-climax.

Very rightly the heat of the writing cools after this, but for a few words at the moment when Frank and Jarvie are about to part from Rob Roy and his wife the passion that animated the account of the lovers' parting recurs. Rob Roy's wife is about to give to Frank a ring that Diana has entrusted to her to pass on as her parting gift and she says as she gives it:

> "This comes from one whom you will never see more. If it is a joyless token, it is well fitted to pass through the hands of one to whom joy can never be known. Her last words were—Let him forget me for ever."
>
> "And can she," I said, almost without being conscious that I spoke, "suppose that is possible?"

That again is Scott speaking from experience. I do not mean that he intrudes a piece of inept autobiography. It is because he has been familiar with this type of feeling that he can make the simplest of words convey so much. Through this familiarity he can use the right artistry; to cause his hero to be so far overcome by the strength of his feelings as to give them away, almost unconsciously, to the company around him. I am reminded of the great passage in *Télémaque*, where the hero, in spite of the immense restraints of aristocratic etiquette, does the same thing.[1] Scott can bore us when he inserts into the love-story of Frank and Diana the stale theme of jealousy through a mistake; but we must not allow that boredom to blind us to the moments when he depicts authentic passion.

I have dwelt on these intense stretches partly to reinforce what I said in the section on *Waverley* about Scott's having it in him to write with an intensity commonly denied him and thereby to enter parts of human experience of which he is commonly thought incapable of entering. But I have dwelt on them also because, issuing so aptly from their context, they add force and beauty to the whole novel. They confirm the existing

[1] I have written on this passage in my *English Epic*, p. 491.

impression that the massive scenes in Glasgow are more than comedy of manners and the violent scenes in the Highlands more than diverting adventure.

I have already admitted the tameness of the concluding scenes in England. It is not difficult to detach them, coming at the end. They need not affect the beautifully contrived motion and the sustained incandescence of the writing throughout most of the rest.

(d) *Reconciliation of Opposing Principles*

I have preferred to write of the art of *Rob Roy* before enlarging on Scott's drastic act of choosing as his grand theme the opposing principles of the new world of commerce and the old world of the clan and the feudal landowner; for only if that theme issues from high art can it make itself felt. Scott gives notice of his theme and then reveals it with subdued emphasis in the English scenes and with powerful emphasis through the actions and the characters in Scotland. When I say 'gives notice', I do not mean that for the moment the reader takes the firm of Osbaldistone and Tresham as more than an unattractive way of life from which Frank insists on escaping. Nevertheless, Scott lodges the theme of commerce in the reader's mind and keeps it there ready to be recollected. More memorable and insistent and indicative are Frank's ruminations when at the Yorkshire inn he meets his first Scotsman (actually Rob Roy in disguise). He then recollects first his nurse's stories of wild doings on the Scottish border and next his father's opinions on Scottish business habits. The firm had large interests in oak-forests in the Highlands, and thought both the owners and their Lowland middlemen tricky to deal with. Here, indeed, is a plain indication, placed in a prominent position, of the novel's double theme. Osbaldistone Hall is on the Scottish border, and Sir Hildebrand and his seven sons, convincingly barren of everything that makes life amiable, and yet satirically reminiscent of the fairy-tale or of Edward III and his family, show what the lawless life of the Border can sink to when it it a senseless survival of an old order and incapable of adapting itself to a new one. Through them Scott meant to convey that in England, the more advanced country, such a survival was more senseless than corresponding survivals in Scotland. So far there is no possible reconciliation. William Osbaldistone, having repudiated barren antiquity, has adopted a modernity in its way as forbidding. The pair of opposites have been powerfully presented in their full mutual hostility.

Soon after the scene has changed to Scotland, the two main characters, main in the amount of attention they attract and in their symbolic functions, meet in Glasgow gaol. Here Rob Roy is at Nicol Jarvie's mercy, as Jarvie will be at Rob's when the scene changes again to the Highlands. Thus we may expect the side of commerce to be dominant in this part. Jarvie is recognised as a great comic creation, and the instinct that impelled Scott to use such a character instead of the conventional hero, for conveying what he most had to say, was his salvation. The period is not long after the Act of Union, and opinion was still bitterly divided about its benefit. Jarvie is the forward-looking man, not the speculative fanatic like William Osbaldistone, but the intelligent and well-disposed realist, who knows how things are going, and who, while making personal capital out of his knowledge, wishes the rest of the community well. Jarvie when confronted with Frank recognises him as "he whom your principal, like an obstinate auld fule, wad make a merchant o', want he or want he no, and the lad turned a strolling stage-player, in pure dislike to the labour an honest man should live by". In other words, commerce is the right life; but opinions differ, and no use forcing a man against his inclinations. And vehemently does Jarvie believe that commerce is the right life, and that Scotland, and Glasgow especially, can live it with the best:

"Na, na, sir, we stand on our ain bottom—we pickle in our ain pock-neuk—We hae our Stirling serges, Musselburgh stuffs. . . . Na, na! let every herring hing by its ain head and every sheep by its ain shank, and ye'll find, sir, us Glasgow folk no sae far ahint but what we may follow."

Scott reserves the culmination in the development of Jarvie till a little before the reader takes leave of him. After he has parted lovingly from his kinsman, Rob, on the shores of Loch

Lomond, he and Frank enter the boat and are rowed down the lake. Frank, soothed by the grandeur of the scenery, but sad at the loss of Diana, thinks how willingly he would live and die a hermit on one of the islands the boat passes:

> The Bailie had also his speculations, but they were of somewhat a different complexion; as I found when, after about an hour's silence, during which he had been mentally engaged in the calculations necessary, he undertook to prove the possibility of draining the lake, and "giving to the plough and harrow many hundred ay, many a thousand acres, from whilk no man could get earthly gude e'enow, unless it were a gedd or a dish of perch now and then".

And part of his project was

> to preserve a portion of the lake just deep enough and broad enough for the purposes of water-carriage, so that coal-barges and gabbards should pass as easily between Dumbarton and Glenfalloch as between Glasgow and Greenock.

The episode is primarily comic, but through the comedy Scott expresses his belief, however reluctant, that the future is largely with the pushing exploiter, the Philistine man of affairs, that you cannot ignore him, that he has his virtues, that he must be fitted into the world of today and tomorrow. And Scott animates his belief through the wonderful character he has built up. Jarvie is overwhelming, unescapable, as a person. But he is not bigoted, he knows the world is varied, and he tolerates people unlike himself. He may be unescapable, but with a part of ourselves we do not want to escape him. He is a man with whom other people can live. He thus contains within himself the means of reconciling to its opposite the principle for which he stands.

Rob Roy is in hopeless and doomed opposition. He is ubiquitous, but he is a mere skirmisher compared with the serried power of his cousin, Nicol Jarvie. He is a Jacobite, he believes in the old type of justice:

> "I give God's malison and mine to a' sort o' magistrates, justices, bailies, sheriffs, sheriffs-officers, constables, and sic-like black cattle, that hae been the plagues o' puir auld Scotland this

hunder year;—it was a merry world when every man held his ain gear wi' his ain grip, and when the country side wasna fashed wi' warrants and poindings and apprizings, and a' that cheatry craft."

Rob's world is the old feudal one, where, as Jarvie put it,

"It's just the laird's command, and the loon maun loup; and the never another law hae they but the length o' their dirks—the broad-sword's pursuer or plaintiff, and the target is defender; the stoutest head bears langest out—and there's a Hieland plea for ye."

But Rob had the special virtues of the way of living that was doomed. Jarvie admits that you can trust his word, that he has "a kind o' Hieland honesty". And he was violent only in self-defence. He was chivalrous towards his enemies and bore no personal spite. Moreover he had been harshly treated and was an outlaw by necessity not choice. Through Rob's embodiment of Highland morality (such as it was) Scott declares that the best of it must be preserved and reconciled with a new way of life. And like Jarvie Rob can allow for another man's opinions. It offended him beyond endurance when Jarvie, in pure goodness of heart, offered to put his boys to a trade as apprentices. It was a dreadful insult, yet Rob restrained himself and allowed the knowledge that Jarvie meant well to prevail. They end in actual harmony, however hopelessly opposed in theory. That harmony is the ultimate meaning of the whole novel.

In *Rob Roy* Scott simultaneously created and expressed the feelings of the body of his countrymen. And they were these: first, Scotland was a country but only in terms of union with England: second, though the sober and mercantile virtues of the Lowlands have inherited the modern world they must be united with the enthusiasms and generosities of the Highland temperament; for differences between peoples and within peoples add to the value of life if they issue in competition and not in conflict, if they enrich and stimulate and do not destroy. In so far as Scott succeeded in saying these things through this great comic novel he was practising the epic mode.

V. S. Pritchett,[1] who does ample justice to Scott's general talent, says that, unlike the Russians, Scott fails to "convey the sense of an abiding destiny going on beyond the characters described". That is true of most of the Waverley Novels, but not of *Rob Roy*, where the characters are more than themselves and stand for principles that reach out beyond them.

(viii) *The 'Heart of Midlothian'*

I can be briefer on the *Heart of Midlothian* because there is no point here in special propaganda. The reputation of the novel is such that if a reader decides to give Scott a proper chance by close and honest reading he will include the *Heart of Midlothian* in his act.

I think it Scott's greatest novel, although the epic quality is less evident than in *Rob Roy*. He wrote for the longest stretches in his most intense and exalted style, and he includes the greatest span of human activity. He makes us feel that men and women of all sorts are dealing with the business of life in many degrees of hope and passivity, of passion and calm, of fanaticism and reasonableness in many places and all at one time. He achieves all the amplitude necessary for the epic. He also wrote with a little-broken mastery. It is a mastery that sometimes makes itself felt in a leisured and simple command of its material; the story appearing to tell itself with no effort, inconspicuous in its absolute propriety. Much of the exposition at the beginning is of this kind. More conspicuously the mastery appears in the places of high passion (and there are more of these than in any other of Scott's novels). In most of them (and I say *most* because there are some places where Scott professes powerful passions and leaves us cold, as in his presentation of Staunton, *alias* Robertson) he has identified himself so thoroughly with his people, has lived himself into the imagined situations so fully, that he never fails to put the right words and the right number of words into the mouths of his speakers. There is something symbolic in his having chosen captions from *Measure for Measure* for three chapters. Not only are those captions much to the point, for Jeanie Deans called

[1] In the *Living Novel* (London 1946), p. 57.

on to perjure herself to save her sister's life is exactly parallel to Isabella called on to sacrifice her chastity to save her brother's life, but they suggest what I believe to be the truth: that Scott's state of mind in composing the greatest scenes in the *Heart of Midlothian* was working like Shakespeare's in the same process; through an uncommon power of self-identification with the men and women in action.

Another thing that points to the *Heart of Midlothian*'s being Scott's masterpiece is the geographical intensity. Scott describes the town of Edinburgh and the country around Arthur's Seat no better than he had described Tully-Veolan in *Waverley*, but he succeeds in impassioning them differently. We associate the Baron and his family with Tully-Veolan in an entirely satisfactory way. But the cottage of Leonard's Crags and Muscat Cairn are, for any reader who has given himself worthily to the book, for ever haunted by the characters who inhabited or frequented those places. Scott did for them what Homer did for the two fountains outside Troy where the women in peace-time used to bring their washing, and what Shakespeare did for Dover Cliff: he made them a piece of their country's, and with that of the world's, mythology.

The *Heart of Midlothian* therefore is, in the quality of some of its parts, better calculated to produce the epic effect than any other novel Scott wrote. What in actual fact is the case?

In some ways Scott gave here his noblest and most powerful version of the great national themes that held his mind. And he did so through the great figure of his heroine. But the novel is not only the heroic story of Jeanie Deans. It is also the old story of the Tale of Two Sisters: as old at least as *Antigone* and repeated in *Arcadia* and the *Vicar of Wakefield*. It is this second story that grows and prevails in the last third of the novel. So doing, it somewhat impairs the clarity of the first theme. Thus it is that Scott's clearest statement of his epic theme is in *Rob Roy*.

Holding in mind the way Scott dealt with his national themes in the earlier novels, we can see that in the *Heart of Midlothian* he once again chose to put the main burden on his protagonist. Indeed, he put a greater burden on her than on either Waverley or Morton. These were mediating figures, the objects of their mediation being outside themselves. Jeanie Deans represents at once one of the sides of the old pair of opposites and a sufficient portion of the other side to effect in her own person the total process. In *Rob Roy* two persons were needed. Now Scott puts all the responsibility in one place. I say nothing of Jeanie Deans as a character in fiction and take it for granted that she is a very great character indeed set in a successfully supporting context. It is only because she is such a character that any political and national significance she can have is more than nominal. Through her Scott best expressed what he thought Scotland was good for. Nicol Jarvie was a huge character, standing for a great measure of Lowland Scotland and looking to the future. But Jeanie is at home over a wider range of society; and, through her heroic acts of saving first her own soul by her refusal to betray her beliefs and second her sister's life by her hazardous journey to London and her resolution in obtaining an interview with the Queen, she enters a realm that belonged more to that of Rob Roy than of Nicol Jarvie. Jarvie, the town merchant, could not have coped with the Duke of Argyle. Jeanie, the peasant, is perfectly at ease with the upper end of the agricultural community. One of the supreme touches in the book is Jeanie's presuming to give the Duke advice. It comes at the end of their first meeting, when the Duke dismisses her and tells her not to be out of the way when he sends.

> Jeanie replied,—"There is little fear of that, sir, for I have little heart to go to see sights amang this wilderness of black houses. But if I might say to your gracious honour, that if ye ever condescend to speak to ony ane that is of greater degree than yoursell, though maybe it is nae civil in me to say sae, just if you would think there can be nae sic odds between you and them, as between poor Jeanie Deans from Saint Leonard's and the Duke of Argyle; and so dinna be chappit back or cast down wi' the first rough answer."

That Jeanie can presume to give advice to the Duke marks her as Scottish, and that alone. No English peasant girl would have added advice to pleadings in that company. But it was not easy thus to presume, and in so doing she speaks for all the thrust and energy of her folk. And the way she speaks combined with what she says expresses that mixture of regard for rank and belief in the rights of the individual which was uniquely characteristic of Scotland.

We must not forget that Jeanie's intervention on her sister's behalf was a solitary heroic and romantic incident. She was a practical woman and a steadily devout woman above everything, and through her Scott acknowledged, as he did through Nicol Jarvie, that it is no use pretending that the trend of the world is not utilitarian. What may save it is the readiness to be heroic when a crisis demands.

After Jeanie has used her peasant eloquence on the Queen and redeemed her sister, she becomes the heroine of a simple success story. She is the good girl who reaps the reward of her goodness by success in this world. It would be tame by itself; but its point is to set off the story of the naughty sister, the clever and beautiful girl whose sins find her out. Effie, saved from hanging, had her chance to reform and to leave her Byronic lover. But she marries him, although marriage means embarking on a life of deceit. She carries the deceit through, at the cost of her peace of mind, but is punished by the knowledge that her illegitimate son is a bandit and by that son's killing his father. Scott made no bones about rewarding virtue and punishing vice in the correct way. But usually he is perfunctory. Only in the *Heart of Midlothian* does he deal genuinely with this conventional theme. It is far and away his most rigidly moral book. Why it should be so puzzles me. Is Scott genuinely caught up in a wave of what one is inclined to call Victorian morality? Is this an instinctive attempt to add to his choric rendering of the genius of Scotland a second choric rendering, that of conventional pietistic morality, professed undoubtedly by the majority of his compatriots? Whatever the answer, the result cannot compare in worth with what he achieved in the first two-thirds of the book. I admire the last third for the job of work it does; it brings, without stint, one part of the action to a full conclusion. It may even "show Scottish life passing into a mellower phase in which old unhappy things are forgotten",[1] though if it mainly does this it takes an unconscionable time over the process. But I cannot

[1] John Buchan, *op. cit.*, p. 188.

escape the conclusion that on the whole it weakens the magnificent achievement in what has gone before.[1]

(ix) *'Ivanhoe'*

Although *Ivanhoe* is Scott's first departure from Scotland and the world he best knew and stands for the preponderance of Neo-Gothic melodrama and historical reconstruction over real life, it retains traces of the great themes that had animated Scott's true epic area. The theme of reconciliation is paramount however much it is overlaid. Antique Saxon and intrusive Norman correspond to Jacobite and Hanoverian, and the conflict between them must be resolved. Wilfrid of Ivanhoe resembles Waverley and Morton in being the symbol and agent of reconciliation. He extends his agency even to the Jews. For about a third of the book the theme is strong: indeed for just as long as Scott retains his absolute mastery over his material and avoids melodrama. And he returns to it explicitly at the end, when Cedric gives up the struggle to make his own race dominant once more and accepts Richard as the joint-ruler of both races. Another resemblance with *Waverley* is through the heroines. Rowena corresponds to Rose, while Rebecca duplicates Flora in her strength of character and in her ending in the nearest Jewish equivalent to the monastic life.

I say these things to suggest not that *Ivanhoe* adds to Scott's epic area but that in continuing the themes that give life to that area it shows how powerful a hold they had on the mind of its author.

(x) *Conclusion*

Whatever their merits, Scott's subsequent Scottish novels do not appreciably enlarge his epic area. You can perceive the old, vital, oppositions in the *Bride of Lammermoor* and the *Legend*

[1] Robin Mayhead in an article on the *Heart of Midlothian* in *Essays in Criticism*, 1956, pp. 266-77, notes that in the first half Scott exploits the theme of what law and justice truly are with much closeness and subtlety. The article shows a welcome change of habit in that it gives Scott a new chance through close reading. But the writer underestimates Scott's seriousness elsewhere, seeing for instance in *Waverley* the seriousness confined to "the picture of the MacIvors and their way of life".

of Montrose, but only by watching for them. The two novels have their virtue as tragic or lively stories in the Neo-Gothic manner. If one could imagine them without their predecessors they would yield further significances. But granted the epic qualities that have gone before, they add nothing. *Redgauntlet* is different. The old Jacobite in Scott genuinely reawakened, and Scott had to exorcise him. He did so in a book of very fluctuating quality. The early correspondence between Darsie Latimer and Alan Fairford and Darsie's journal alternate between extreme tedium and extreme vividness. In describing the Solway Firth Scott writes at his height. The action quickens rather more than half-way through, and the structural concentration through which everything converges on the scenes in Crackenthorp's Inn cannot be praised too highly. General Colin Campbell as *deus ex machina* has the dignity of impersonal fate. It is useless, we agree, for the rebels to kick against the pricks. But however much Redgauntlet and the rest stand for an impossible and outworn past, and Colin Campbell for the irresistible tide of new events, I am not impelled to connect this presentation of the old theme with the earlier ones. In the early group Scott was forming and expressing the innermost *ethos* of his countrymen, in *Redgauntlet* he was working something out of his system.

It should have become evident in the course of what I have written that Scott has the amplitude necessary for the epic and that he attempts to express large sentiments held by a great group of people, and that his deficiency is in organisation, in the prolonged exercise of the conscious will. He functions explosively through a succession of outbursts of the creative genius. He planned and executed no single work so closely that it contained nothing superfluous and expressed the sum of all he was good for. To revert to my beginning, he remains, in spite of three considerable volcanic eminences, an epic area.

What chance is there of Scott's getting his due, which he certainly does not in spite of the exhortations of some eminent recent critics? I suppose it is because the general public has got out of the way of reading him aright, while the more academic connoisseurs of the novel favour the more rigorous standards suggested by the practice of Flaubert and James.

Judged solely by those standards, Scott fares ill enough. For all his relish of the banquet of life Scott is shown up as deplorably diffuse. In fact, he behaves like a monkey given a meal of potatoes. The monkey takes up a potato, smells it, takes a bite, throws it away; takes a second, rubs it on the back of his head, takes a bite, throws it away. And so on with the rest; he won't make a job of any single one. Think what Scott misses over Diana Vernon's psychology, what a neglected wealth of potential interest there is in her character, in her thwarted high spirits finding an outlet, *faute de mieux*, in Jacobite intrigue. Or think of the ease with which Waverley and Fergus are allowed to be drawn together. What an absence of subtlety and thoroughness in analysing their motives. How pitifully unexplained too is Effie Deans's seduction by Robertson.

But how does James fare when judged by the standards of Scott? He becomes niggling, skulking. He is rootless, expatriate, a mental eunuch, without patriotism or personal passion. Helpless in the immediate business of life, he is incapable of sharing in it like a man and treats it at second hand, as mere 'copy' for his art. And in the methods of that art, if Scott is a monkey, James is the valetudinarian chew-chew, who, having taken a bite, masticates it *ad nauseam* and will not swallow or reject it till it has lost every trace of its savour. By the side of Scott's fullbloodedness James shows up pale and contemptible.

Both sets of strictures are monstrously false, and why justice cannot be done to both authors simultaneously I personally find it hard to understand. Nevertheless, I know that criticism has been and always will be the prey of the partisan spirit. Many people cannot feel warmly in favour of one kind of art without ignoring or despising its opposite. Admiring Shelley they hated Pope; discovering Donne they found Spenser's expansiveness damnable. Not all critics join the hubbub. Hazlitt pleaded that if you wanted certain literary qualities you could find them better in Pope than elsewhere. Spenser has had his champions. I would plead that a select number of Scott's novels are due for renewed recognition as great literature without the least wish to decry the virtues of a more inspissated kind of fiction.

5

Interlude

(i)

I DO not find any novels of the epic kind between the *Heart of Midlothian* (1818) and *Nostromo* (1904). But I cannot pass over this long period without saying why I omit certain novels that might on the surface demand inclusion. It would be foolish to review all the major novels in those ninety years, explaining why I do not include them. To demonstrate that *Wuthering Heights* was not an epic, when no sane person would begin suggesting that it was, would be to waste words. Not all cases are so clear as this one, and I shall not have contented all readers by my omissions. But I have chosen to consider five novels either on my own judgement or in deference to what recent critics have said. Of these I have held back one, *Middlemarch*, because it offers so instructive a contrast with the *Old Wives' Tale* that I cannot forbear grouping the two books together. The other four can be fitly considered separately.

(ii) *Thackeray: 'Vanity Fair'*

Among Thackeray's novels *Vanity Fair* has the largest scope, doing greatest justice to its author's capacities; it has thence the best initial chance of touching the epic.

Amplitude of a kind it has. The characters have all the room they want to move about in; and Thackeray insists on working out their destinies without stint or hurry. He can bore us with this insistence, and yet we admire and approve his thoroughness. Thus, when Becky has suffered her great fall and goes into exile on the Continent, Thackeray refuses to allow the waning of interest, inevitable after this catastrophe, to panic him, to force him into the least hurry. He had centred interest in Becky's gamble and Rawdon's shifting part in it and had made it impossible to kindle the book into its former intensity, once the issue of that gamble was declared. Nevertheless, he goes on manfully working up and out the things to which he has been committed. We know that Dobbin will get his Amelia, and with one part of ourselves we deplore the drawing out of the process. With another part of ourselves we admire Thackeray's insistence on allowing plenty of room. Painfully he constructs a new setting, the petty capital town of Pumpernickel, in which to transact the things he is pledged to. Neither setting nor transactions can stir us like their predecessors; yet they make their impression. Amelia and Dobbin develop unguessed ingredients of their characters and give the lie to those readers who have called them static. Amelia unexpectedly tyrannises over Dobbin; and Dobbin as unexpectedly revolts. It is this revolt which, at long last, makes a new climax: one for which we are grateful and which leaves its substantial mark on our minds. And, finally, the very delay until the revelation of George Osborne's long-preserved love-letter to Becky in Brussels urging elopement brings the plot to rest gives the last pages a special zest. A moderate boredom, we agree, has not been too heavy a price to pay for the admirably ample space Thackeray has allowed for his conclusion.

But amplitude of method need not imply amplitude of the things to which the method is applied. There is amplitude in the way Jonson works out *Volpone*; but its substance cannot claim that quality. It would be wrong to call the world of *Vanity Fair* narrow, for the largeness of some of the characters precludes any such thought. But Thackeray does not animate many strata of society—fewer than Fielding does in *Tom Jones* —indeed he is rather puzzled by his age than familiar with it in depth. Thus limited, he cannot voice its 'accepted unconscious metaphysic'.

Nor does Thackeray achieve an epic effect through the inclusiveness and symbolic effect of his characters. It would be vain to argue that Becky and Amelia cover through their contrasted natures and careers as great an area of the human mind as Arnold Bennett meant Constance and Sophia Baines to cover in the *Old Wives' Tale*. Each in her way is too extreme; and anyhow Becky dwarfs her opposite. If Becky is truly paired with anyone, it is with her own husband, Rawdon Crawley.

It is this pairing and the supremacy of the pair that should inform us that the literary kind to which *Vanity Fair* most nearly belongs is not the epic but the picaresque romance. *Vanity Fair*, even if much nobler, is the logical heir of *Barry Lyndon*, which it succeeded in time. Becky and Rawdon are both adventurers and for a while they join in preying on society. They are also among the select repertory of the major characters in world fiction. In every other way they differ. And this diversity-in-likeness gives the novel its own richness as well as its master motive. The picaresque story, as I said in my opening chapter, is a genuine literary kind because it is based on a permanent proclivity of human nature; the proclivity to sympathise with anti-social behaviour while knowing that it cannot go on for ever. Falstaff and his rejection are its most famous expression in English. The careers of Rawdon and Becky furnish a superb example of it. We want Becky to win her gambles, until Rawdon develops a human affection and the beginning of a moral sense. Then we waver, and Rawdon becomes the successful agent of a transfer of feelings which many people still believe Shakespeare to have failed at when he made Falstaff lose his gamble.

There is also a good deal of support for the central item, the adventures of Becky and Rawdon. There are other adventurers besides themselves. Old Osborne is the successful adventurer in business; the self-made man. Joe Sedley, timid as he is, adventures for money in India. Young Osborne is the *parvenu* among the aristocrats who fill the commissions in the British Army. Most of the characters are or have been on the make and they unite to give the novel its special character. The disinterestedness of Amelia and Dobbin is a smaller affair and serves as a foil rather than forms the main substance. There can be no question of *Vanity Fair's* being an epic; it remains the superlative picaresque romance.

(iii) *Melville: 'Moby Dick'*

To observe that *Moby Dick* was published only three years after *Vanity Fair* has the air of being both senseless and wantonly sensational. It does no good to put these works together;

the one does nothing to enlighten the other; and the contemporaneity of the two appears less as a truth than as a joke in doubtful taste on the part of fortune. Nevertheless the novels, however different, have a reach and a boldness that force us to inquire whether they are of the epic kind.

On the surface *Moby Dick* might well be the choric expression of the world's multitude of men living dangerously and close to nature and unencumbered by women. It could even be maintained that Ahab, among other things, symbolises the canalisation of energies and the isolation from the norm of human living that such a life imposes as its penalty. Nonetheless he is apt to his context: he may live apart from the rest of his ship's crew; yet not more than that crew lives from the majority of men who lead more stable and more variedly social lives. If he exists apart, to hunt one whale in particular, the men he commands have a vocation as sharply severed from those of the generality as the miner's vocation underground.

However, Melville has not grasped and realised the choric potentiality. For one thing, his technique of alternating whale-lore with action ends by growing monotonous and mechanical. The spinning out, acceptable up to a point, lowers the pitch, weakens the intensity. We are not convinced that the author is not inflating his theme, is not giving it a bulk it cannot properly bear. Then the three ship's officers are not memorable enough figures to bear a great weight of meaning. For the book to create the epic effect it was absolutely necessary that these major characters should cover between them a large area of the human spirit, and that their different temperaments should be clearly and cogently displayed. Only so could the reader acquire the confidence that the author is qualified to speak for men as well as for himself. It is true that Starbuck makes a considerable impression and Stubb some. But Flask makes none at all; he is a superfluity. We have only to compare Melville's trio with the brothers Karamazov to see their comparative poverty.

Moby Dick, though a great book, remains something of an oddity. It is individual, not choric. It reflects the spirit of a great and strange man, but it does not interpret the 'accepted unconscious metaphysic' of a group.

(iv) *Henry James*

There would be no occasion to bring in Henry James but for recent efforts to draw attention to two of his least popular novels. I cannot see anyone asserting that his best loved work, whether an early success like the *Portrait of a Lady* or a late success like the *Ambassadors*, touches the epic kind. That work, however much it includes of the tragic, of melodrama, of the *macabre*, or of a sense of encircling doom, is true to the general idiom of comedy. The element it inhabits is the world of manners with its superimposed and yet interpenetrating social planes; and, however much talk there is about the fineness of this or that character, we see them achieving not a religious or existential adjustment to the total scheme of things but a thought-out surrender to the ineluctible conditions of their social setting. Even Milly in the *Wings of the Dove* is not a fully tragic character; rather she is deprived at a stroke of the social setting to which she was singularly well attuned and which she could have signally adorned. The wall she faces as she turns away is a blank, not a new, tragic, situation. Corrupt as are all four main characters in the *Golden Bowl*—corrupt either in themselves or in their submission to the acts that are in a way forced upon them—intolerable in its cruelty as is the fate of Charlotte Stant, the total novel owes its allegiance, if anywhere, to the comic norm, to the laws of the way of the world, or, if you like, to the principle declared by Chaucer at the beginning of the *Miller's Tale*:

> But sith that he was fallen in the snare
> He moste endure, *as oother folk*, his care.

Intensity within the comic norm, detail heaped-up within a limited psychological area and serving ultimately to make more striking the long hidden and, when revealed, startlingly simple situations or states of mind, and not the epic amplitude or the choric convictions of multitudes, are the qualities of Henry James's best loved fiction.

But in 1886, when he was forty-three years old, the age when he should be both mature and at the height of his natural energy, after his early success with the *Portrait of a Lady* and before the beginning of his later successes with the *Spoils of Poynton*, he published two novels said to be in a different category from the rest on account of their political content. They are the *Bostonians* and the *Princess Casamassima*. They cost Henry James a great deal, he thought them his best work up to date, and he was sanguine of their success. At the time of publication they fell flat and till recently have been among the least read of his novels. But in the *Liberal Imagination* Trilling has written brilliantly on their behalf, claiming for the second of the two a high eminence. Leavis has claimed a similar eminence for the *Bostonians*. Putting together this possible eminence and the political themes, I can hardly ignore the chance that in these novels James was trying something new and that the novelty was of the epic kind.

The *Bostonians* tells the story of a girl with a fine appetite for life, a sweet nature, and a gift of oratory, but with little will and no ideas of her own, fought over by a grim spinster devoted to the cause of women's rights and a tough and ambitious war-veteran from the South. But the political theme of women's rights is setting not substance. It is not solid in its own right and merely serves as the stage for social comedy and purely personal predicaments. The book is good in its way till the end, when the hero, in the romantic part (with a difference) of Young Lochinvar, intercepts the heroine about to address an enormous meeting in the Music Hall at Boston. The episode is exciting but inept and it ruins the high comedy that has been so beautifully built up. But even if the book had succeeded in its way throughout, that way had nothing to do with the epic.

The *Princess Casamassima* cannot be dismissed so shortly. The anarchist politics it includes count for much more than the feminist politics of the *Bostonians*. Trilling has shown how Henry James, though lacking any considerable, let alone expert, knowledge of the revolutionary politics of his time, does in fact present them with great accuracy. More important, he gives them life. When he makes Paul Muniment, the most serious of the anarchists, refrain from condemning the 'haves' for having, while coolly set on taking what they have, he wins our complete assent. We agree that a real revolutionary would feel like that. When he pictures his formidable cockney beauty, Millicent Henning, as the proletarian singer of the new Marseillaise he achieves a convincing stroke of the imagination. Not only does James make the anarchist politics live, but Trilling may be right when he claims for the novel a wide historical significance. He says:

> It is a novel which has at its very center the assumption that Europe has reached the full of its ripeness and is passing over into rottenness, that the peculiarly beautiful light it gives forth is in part the reflection of a glorious past and in part the phosphorescence of a present decay, that it may meet its end by violence and that this is not wholly unjust, although never before has the old sinful continent made so proud and pathetic an assault upon our affections.

Many people have glanced at or contemplated or agonised over the notion of the decline of the West; and it is not out of the question that James was the mouthpiece of this multitude. He may in fact have achieved the choric effect necessary for the epic. Further (in spite of the concentration on a highly specialised kind of politics) James presents us with a wealth of character situated at widely different points on the social scale. And they are given space and breadth by their most genuine abode in a great city. A good case could be made out for the novel's amplitude, an amplitude unique in James's work.

However good the initial case for the novel's touching the epic, it soon collapses when put to further test. Trilling has seen how personal to the author was the mental struggle to which one of the twin protagonists, Hyacinth Robinson, was exposed, the struggle (to put it in its most general terms) between the claims of art and action:

> When, then, we find Henry James creating for his Hyacinth a situation in which he must choose between action and the fruits of the creative spirit of Europe, we cannot but see that he has placed at the center of his novel a matter whose interest is of the most personal kind.

The matter, which included what I have just called the decline of the West, was personal in more than one way. It was, as it were, endemic in the James family; and it became acutely practical when the American Civil War began. If through Hyacinth, destroyed by the conflicting claims of political violence and the beauty of the thing he is committed to kill, James eased and objectified his personal conflicts, it does not mean that he thereby compromised his artistic integrity. He may have made a perfectly good work of art. But it does mean that he used politics not for themselves but as a means; they are a secondary not a primary subject. In confirmation of this, note how externally James presents his most powerful political figure, Paul Muniment. He never makes us see things through Paul's eyes, thus keeping him after all a peripheral figure. And in the end, true to life as the politics may be and animated by their personal application, they resemble the feminism of the *Bostonians* in that their main task is to set off high comedy. Comedy, not tragedy; for, though so much of the book concerns Hyacinth's predicament and his ultimate defeat by it, James carefully keeps Hyacinth's scale small (the very name tells us as much) and our feelings about him confined to the less intense world of pathos and this side the intenser one of tragedy. Moreover, Hyacinth takes part in the great comic episodes that are the backbone of the novel along with another figure of pathos, Lady Aurora. Stronger than his interest in politics is James's delight in the delicacies of the social scene, in the English form of snobbery, as when he makes Hyacinth, in spite of his slum breeding, see that Lady Aurora, who has shed all pride of class and bows down in reverence to poverty, might yet find the Princess herself not quite a lady. And, after all, the book takes its name not from the brave, pathetic little man who missed being truly tragic but from a richly comic figure, the lovely American girl married to the wealthy Italian prince. Her vitality and charm are prodigious and she can keep up her vagaries with intense energy for a long time; but not quite long enough. Thus when, having sought the dinginess of Madeira Place as her home to demonstrate the seriousness of her concern with the revolution, she is shown in her sitting-room reading a heavy volume on capital and labour, she becomes exquisitely ludicrous. And Madeira Place is the scene of a classic comic situation: the deserted husband and Hyacinth (now ousted by Paul Muniment from the place of chief political confidant of the Princess) watching from a dark corner the cab deposit Paul and the Princess at the door of her lodging. The Princess herself is in the great line of the comic victim who "moste endure, as oother folk, his care". She has chosen to attempt things a little beyond her powers, great as these are, and we know that she will have to learn her lesson and to conform to the way of the world. And she receives her lesson when near the end of the book Paul tells her that she will go back to her husband and that her most useful contribution to the great cause has been the money she has given it. Here lies the centre of the book, and not either in Hyacinth's suicide or in the political themes. Thus orientated, the *Princess Casamassima* does not touch the epic in any place whatever.

6

Conrad: 'Nostromo'

It is the bitter fate of any idea to lose its royal form and power, to lose its 'virtue' the moment it descends from its solitary throne to work its will among the people.

(CONRAD, *Autocracy and War*, 1905)

(i) *Its Prominence*

IT is not surprising that *Nostromo*, published in 1904, was not at once recognised for the great thing it is. As an adventure-story it was disturbingly depressing, as a picture of life it offended current notions of human progress, and by being greatly different from everything Conrad had written already it disappointed the expectations of most of the readers that he had accumulated up to that point. We are no longer put off by the two first prejudices and we are growing convinced that *Nostromo* is Conrad's greatest novel; but we still make it too much like some of its predecessors and ignore portions of the great wealth it offers us. Even those who have written best on Conrad have limited its scope unduly. I will give an example.

Douglas Hewitt's *Conrad: a Reassessment*[1] as a whole is a close and acute piece of criticism. But he would reduce Conrad to a too precise and limited set of formulas. To characterise Conrad in the great period of his early maturity, the period of *Lord Jim*, the *Heart of Darkness*, *Falk*, *Nostromo*, and the *Secret Sharer*, he uses the familiar distinction between the expansive novel that sprawls out into society and the contracting novel that concentrates inwards on the hero, usually tragic. And he finds all these of the second type: all, in Conrad's own phrase, "free from land entanglements". Their heroes, against the habit of most Victorian fiction, are truly central, like the hero of tragic drama; they dominate their surroundings; there is no inter-

[1] Cambridge 1952.

ference from outside. And the technique suits the requirements of the absorbent hero: everything is tied in; there are no accidental visitors or even accidental objects. However right Hewitt may here be over the *Heart of Darkness*, he is largely wrong over *Nostromo*. The very virtue of *Nostromo* is that it combines the austere soul-searchings of the absorbent tragic hero (or rather heroes) with a great deal of 'land entanglement'; that, after the manner of the *Iliad*, it pictures not only man's private struggles with his destiny but also a whole phase of man's political and social life. However closely tied together the parts of *Nostromo* may be, it is immensely suggestive of issues wider than that of the hero's predicament. That Conrad can suggest so much through so incredibly concatenated a plot is precisely his triumph.

(ii) *Its Span*

To leave the critics and turn to the novel, the first thing that should be evident is that it is unique among all the works of Conrad in its span, both of space and of time. It concentrates on an imagined small town in Central or South America but simultaneously it makes us aware of the whole world outside. The main action takes place within three days, but simultaneously is set in a great stretch of history with hints of prehistory or of the fabulous. These matters are vital in creating the epic effect.

(a) *In Place*

To begin with the dimension of place. Costaguana is much more than the self-contained and narrow setting which Conrad sometimes uses to correspond to and set off the stripped and fundamental conflicts of a few characters; a ship or the abandoned quay in *Victory*. Costaguana is full of a seething and varied life, and its fortunes are the concern of much of the world outside. It is ruthlessly faithful to the virtues and vices of Spanish America, but it is exposed to the inroads and the criticisms of some of the chief nations of the earth. Through these inroads and these criticisms Conrad not only tells us more of Spanish America but conveys a whole phase of

Western European policy and thought. The following passage illustrates (as could a score of others) this double operation. It describes Charles Gould returning to his house at dawn of the third day of rioting at Sulaco:

> Charles Gould rode on, and turned into the archway of his house. In the patio littered with straw, a practicante, one of Dr Monygham's native assistants, sat on the ground with his back against the rim of the fountain, fingering a guitar discreetly, while two girls of the lower class, standing up before him, shuffled their feet a little and waved their arms, humming a popular dance tune. Most of the wounded during the two days of rioting had been taken away already by their friends and relations, but several figures could be seen sitting up balancing their bandaged heads in time to the music. Charles Gould dismounted. A sleepy mozo coming out of the bakery door took hold of the horse's bridle; the practicante endeavoured to conceal his guitar hastily; the girls, unabashed, stepped back smiling; and Charles Gould, on his way to the staircase, glanced into a dark corner of the patio at another group, a mortally wounded Cargador with a woman kneeling by his side; she mumbled prayers rapidly, trying at the same time to force a piece of orange between the stiffening lips of the dying man.
>
> The cruel futility of things stood unveiled in the levity and sufferings of that incorrigible people; the cruel futility of lives and of deaths thrown away in the vain endeavour to attain an enduring solution of the problem.[1]

That is Spanish America seen through the eyes of a certain Englishman; and many other eyes see it. But though it exists thus contingently, as it meets the outside world, it exists also, and as firmly, in its own rights. And that outside world too has the same double function. It serves first as background and influence. It is *there*, while the fierce action proceeds at Sulaco; and it intervenes to direct that action. But it exists in its own right too. It presents what were for Conrad the main political drifts of the late nineteenth century. Of these I shall write later. My present point is that by combining the closely in-bred, the strictly documented domestic, with the ecumenical *Nostromo* achieves the kind of variety and amplitude propitious to the epic effect.

[1] pp. 363-4.

(b) *In History*

In point of time, though much of the action is transacted within the compass of three days, we learn a very great deal about roughly the amount of time (before and after those days) that a man could be conscious of in an ordinary lifetime. And into that time a whole revolution in the ways of life is compressed; feudalism yields to the pressure and the exploitations of modern capitalism, which itself becomes exposed to the beginnings of a communist movement. Such scope is impressive enough, but it is not the whole, for the revolution, propelled ultimately by western Europe with the help of North America and not by the Spaniards of the new world, repeats a pattern set up hundreds of years ago.

Conrad set the action of *Nostromo* in the context of history with engaging tact. He scarcely ever moralises like the historian, but works mainly through a judicious modicum of plain but pregnant facts about the condition of the land in the old colonial days. The road from Sulaco to Rincon and into the plain is still the old royal road, the Camino Real; and the gentle iteration of the name works secretly on our minds. And there is the statue of Charles IV at the entrance of the Alameda, now known to the ignorant simply as the Horse of Stone. The San Tomé mine itself had a long history. In the earliest Spanish days it was worked by slave labour, as in its latest phase it was to be worked by men nominally free but subject to different forms of compulsion. In the interval it was closed, and then reopened after the war of independence by English exploiters. These were murdered in the confused times after the death of Guzman Bento, the savage dictator. The new governments confiscated and owned the mine but could not work it, and one of them forced it on Gould's father in repayment for the loans it had wrung from him. Charles Gould, inheriting and working it, suffered yet another version of the slavery it had been destined to inflict from the day of its opening. He is but one of a number of historic victims. Nor were royal road and mine the only witnesses of a cruel past.

The heavy stonework of bridges and churches left by the conquerors proclaimed the tribute-labour of vanished nations.

The power of king and church was gone, but at the sight of some heavy ruinous pile overtopping from a knoll the low mud walls of a village, Don Pépé would interrupt the tale of his campaigns to exclaim—

"Poor Costaguana! Before, it was everything for the Padres, nothing for the people; and now it is everything for those great politicos in Sta. Marta, for negroes and thieves."

Writing his letter to his sister about the progress of the riots, Decoud tells her that Viola's house, in which he writes, "may have been contrived by a Conquistador farmer of the pearl fishery three hundred years ago". And it is Decoud who utters the most explicit statement of history repeating itself. The Goulds and their party, which includes Decoud, are returning in their carriage from the harbour where they have seen Barrios and his troops (armed with the rifles Decoud has just brought from Europe) embark for Cayta. As the carriage passes through the "old gateway facing the harbour like a shapeless monument of leaves and stones", their ears are smitten by a "strange, piercing shriek", and the whole procession of people from the harbour turn their heads to see an empty construction train "returning from the Campo to the palisaded yards". The driver applies his brakes,

> and when the ear-splitting screech of the steam-whistle for the brakes had stopped, a series of hard, battering shocks, mingled with the clanking of chain-couplings, made a tumult of blows and shaken fetters under the vault of the gate.[1]

These words end a chapter; and their emphatic place confirms Hewitt's surmise[2] that these fetters are symbolic of the grip on the land of Costaguana maintained by the new railway, a principal instrument of those 'material interests' whose triumph is one of the themes of the book. Anyhow, immediately after, in the next chapter, Decoud takes them as such. The carriage passes through the gate: with the noise of whistle and of shaken couplings in his ears he scanned

> moodily the inner aspect of the gate. The squat turreted sides held up between them a mass of masonry with bunches of grass growing at the top, and a grey, heavily scrolled, armorial shield

[1] p. 172.　　　　　　　　　[2] *Op. cit.*, p. 84.

of stone above the apex of the arch with the arms of Spain nearly smoothed out as if in readiness for some new device typical of the impending progress.

And the combination of sound and sight provoke him to remark that the "sound puts a new edge on a very old truth". And that truth is that Spanish America was subject from the first to the invasions of the English. The new, English, railway is a later version of an old story. Decoud explains:

"Just imagine our forefathers in morions and corselets drawn up outside this gate, and a band of adventurers just landed from their ships in the harbour there. Thieves, of course. Speculators, too. Their expeditions, each one, were the speculations of grave and reverend persons in England. . . . But to return to my noises; there used to be in the old days the sound of trumpets outside that gate. War trumpets! I'm sure they were trumpets. . . . In those days this town was full of wealth. Those men came to take it. Now the whole land is like a treasure-house, and all these people are breaking into it, whilst we are cutting each other's throats. . . . It has always been the same. We are a wonderful people, but it has always been our fate to be exploited."

And in the end Charles Gould, who thought he had accepted the burden of the mine from the highest motives (and was indeed partly right in his thought), slips into the mood of an adventurer, the English adventurer on foreign soil:

After all, with his English parentage and English upbringing he perceived that he was an adventurer in Costaguana. . . . He was prepared, if need be, to blow up the whole San Tomé mountain sky high out of the territory of the Republic. This resolution expressed the tenacity of his character . . . and something, too, of the spirit of a buccaneer throwing a lighted match into the magazine rather than surrender his ship.[1]

Like the English-staffed railway, Gould, in the end, "puts a new edge on a very old truth".

Through this insistence on the setting of history, never obtruded but beautifully contrived and sufficiently sustained, *Nostromo* achieves a breadth and a dignity unique in Conrad's novels and through that achievement shares in the virtues of the epic kind.

[1] pp. 365-6.

(c) *Fairy-lore*

But Conrad does not limit his sense of time to recorded history, for *Nostromo* as well as being centred fiercely in the reality of modern life is a fairy-tale; and the fairy-tale extends the options of time through the whole span of datable human events to the unknown or purely conjectural; it unites the nearest and the farthest.

As far as I know, the fairy-tale element in *Nostromo* has passed undetected: a surprising omission when one considers how fashionable such a detection is. Anyhow, since it has so passed, I had better go to some length in trying to establish that it is indeed there. What first put me on to it was the behaviour of General Montero, destined later to lead the revolt against the Ribierist government, at the lunch given on board the *Juno* to President Dictator Ribiera himself, others of his government, and Sir John, who had come from Europe "to smooth the path for his railway". Montero is incensed that he is not getting enough attention. "Why was it that nobody was looking at him?"—at him who had performed the "greatest military exploit of modern times". He is a sinister figure:

> The white plume, the coppery tint of his broad face, the blue-black of the moustaches under the curved beak, the mass of gold on sleeves and breast, the high shining boots with enormous spurs, the working nostrils, the imbecile and domineering stare of the glorious victor of Rio Seco had in them something ominous and incredible; the exaggeration of a cruel caricature, the fatuity of solemn masquerading, the atrocious grotesqueness of some military idol of Aztec conception and European bedecking, awaiting the homage of worshippers.

Like the railway and Charles Gould, Montero repeats early South American history, but just as surely he is the malicious fairy, slighted, resentful, and bent on mischief, at the christening feast of the infant railway. Once we see Montero in this guise (and Conrad leaves us here to our own inferences) we find the fairy theme, with its kin the ballad theme all over the place, often explicitly mentioned.

The world of magic enters immediately after the opening

paragraphs introducing the setting of Sulaco, for the barren peninsula of Azuera, which bounds the gulf on the north, "is deadly because of its forbidden treasures". True, there is no dragon guarding them, but they belong to the class that dragons used to be interested in. And the devils and ghosts that do this work are a satisfactory substitute. Many adventurers perished looking for the gold, the latest being two foreign sailors, probably American; and it matters that they should be so, for it is thus that Conrad unites present reality with a fabulous past. This opening legend is like a dumb show in Elizabethan drama, shadowing future happenings; for the mine which Gould inherits is fabulous also, as is the boat-load of silver that corrupts Nostromo. Gould's father, we are told, "became at once mine-ridden. . . . It took the form of the Old Man of the Sea fastened upon his shoulders. He began also to dream of vampires." His letters to his son had the flavour of "a gruesome Arabian Nights tale". Charles Gould, intellectually convinced that it is his duty to take on the responsibility of working the mine for the general good, retains a superstitious fear because in so taking it on he goes against his father's wishes. As the mine is exploited, its wealth begins to grow fabulous: "there had never been anything in the world to approach the vein of the Gould Concession". It reminds one of the Cave of Mammon in Spenser. It ends by being far more than a big silver mine for "its territory, containing gold, silver, copper, lead, cobalt, extends for miles along the foot-hills of the Cordillera".

Charles Gould, the book's principal hero, is the exiled prince, the son of a king who has been robbed of his inheritance. When his father dies he returns to claim it. He succeeds, and the people habitually call him the King of Sulaco. Decoud, who stands outside the fairy-tale and lives in his intellect and in the single canalised appetite of love alone, dislikes Gould in his part of fairy prince and remarks of him that "he could not believe his own motives if he did not make them first a part of some fairy-tale", and again that for Gould and by no means for himself life is a "moral romance derived from the tradition of a pretty fairy-tale". If Montero is the wicked fairy at the feast, Mrs Gould is the good fairy, as Conrad keeps telling us.

For instance, this is how she appears, early in the book, in her drawing-room:

> Mrs Gould, with her little head and shining coils of hair, sitting in a cloud of muslin and lace before a slender mahogany table, resembled a fairy posed lightly before dainty philtres dispensed out of vessels of silver and porcelain.

But it is a fairy-tale with a tragic turn. The good fairy fails to get the reward due to her for helping the prince to his inheritance. A wall of silver encloses him and keeps them apart, and it has been "erected by evil spirits". And in the end she suffers a species of defeat:

> Small and dainty, as if radiating a light of her own in the deep shade of the interlaced boughs, she resembled a good fairy, weary with a long career of well-doing, touched by the withering suspicion of the uselessness of her labours, the powerlessness of her magic.

And her defeat is made the more bitter by the fabulous wealth the prince's inheritance has brought her: she is "wealthy beyond great dreams of wealth".

If Gould is the exiled prince, Nostromo is the proletarian, the swineherd's son or the scullion, who achieves wealth by his courage and resourcefulness. But like Gould he deals with enchanted things and there is an initial curse on his traffic with the silver of the mine. He has nothing to do with the mine itself, but is brought in touch with a boat-load of silver from it. Once so brought, he is never free from its enchantment. He begins his dealings with it in the unnatural darkness that invests the Golfo Placido at night.

> The eye of God Himself could not find out what work a man's hand is doing in there; and you would be free to call the devil to your aid with impunity if even his malice were not defeated by such a blind darkness.

From the first Nostromo feels superstitiously about the load of silver. He tells the dying Teresa that he is needed to save it and that it is "a greater treasure than the one they say is guarded by ghosts and devils in Azuera". He has to choose between fulfilling his promise to save the silver and obeying the request of the dying Teresa to fetch her a priest. In denying that request (as Gould disobeyed his father's order to keep clear of the mine), Nostromo corrupted his conscience and, becoming desperate, ended by selling his soul for the whole load of silver. The whole load; because, as Dr Monygham remarked, "for taking the curse of death on my back, as you call it, nothing else but the whole treasure would do". Actually, Nostromo does not get the whole load, for Decoud took four ingots as weights to ensure his drowning when he jumped overboard. Conrad does not pursue this theme, but plainly, if he had wished to end the story of Nostromo happily, he could have used the missing ingots as a means of his escape. Not having received full payment, Nostromo could have repudiated his bargain and expelled the alien soul that had taken possession of him. Anyhow, the four missing ingots, as well as being the entirely realistic means of ensuring the death of an unenchantable character, come from the very heart of fairy-lore.

It would be tedious to list other references to fairies, ghosts, and enchantment. There are plenty more. Conrad's triumph is that he has integrated his fairy-lore so beautifully with the whole complex of the book that readers have deeply felt rather than consciously perceived it. I have said that by introducing the themes of the fairy-tale Conrad extended the dimension of his novel's imagined time; simultaneously he enriched the novel's content incalculably.

(iii) *Human Variety*

So far I have put the great variety of *Nostromo* mainly in terms of place and time. But the human variety is just as great. Conrad is at home equally with idealist and scoundrel, with audacity and cowardice, with simple and complex people. Sotillo refusing to believe that the silver has eluded him or torturing Hirsch is not less real than the old Garibaldino watching the snows of Higuerota. The temporising Ribierists remaining behind at Sulaco and drawing up their memorandum for the invading rebels under Pedro Montero are as real as Charles Gould, who suggests they would act with greater dignity if they retired to their houses and awaited the

event. The complexity of Dr Monygham convinces as much
as the simplicity of Captain Mitchell. But Conrad's greatest
triumph (in spite of, or rather in addition to the fabulous
element) is that he creates the illusion of life being lived all at
once by a great number of very different people. He does this
partly by his technique of passing backward and forward in
time, thereby removing from the reader all temptation to thin
out events by stringing them on a long chain. But he does it
also by his miraculous power of keeping everything and all
people present simultaneously in his head. And he reveals that
power through the sheer wealth of unexpected small touches,
touches we are absolutely certain were not contrived casually
on the spur of the moment but are minute and highly significant revelations of all the more permanent wealth that lies
beneath them. It is the same power that Homer commands in
the *Iliad* when he suddenly mentions the insignificant military
class of store-keepers or tells us that Patroclus's captive maid-
servants, when they lamented his death, were in reality
lamenting their own unhappy lot. Conrad is in complete command of the total life of his Sulaco, not to speak of life outside
it. As an example of his significant revelations, take Nostromo's
account of the old woman looking for her son during the riots:

> She is one of those old women that you find in this country at
> the back of huts, crouching over fireplaces, with a stick on the
> ground by their side, and almost too feeble to drive away the
> stray dogs from their cooking-pots.

Or take a couple of touches in one of the greatest moments of
the book: the moment when all the bells in Sulaco break out
into a concerted violence of din to welcome the entry of the
rebel Monterists and the whole staff of the Casa Gould pour
out of their quarters, terrified, into the patio. It was then that
"Charles Gould beheld all the extent of his domestic establishment, even to the gatekeeper". This half-paralysed old man
had been the personal servant of Gould's uncle, present when
his master was shot by Bento's men, and Gould had taken him
into his establishment.

> Charles Gould noted particularly the big patriarchal head of
> that witness in the rear of the other servants. But he was surprised

to see a shrivelled old hag or two, of whose existence within the walls of his house he had not been aware. They must have been the mothers, or even the grandmothers, of some of his people. There were a few children, too, more or less naked, crying and clinging to the legs of their elders. He had never before noticed any sign of a child in his patio.[1]

Gould may not have known the existence of these people, but Conrad did, and long before he thought fit to mention them. That mention indeed is a wonderful stroke, quite unexpected and bearing the imprint of absolute truth. These secret hangers-on of the great house are, after an instant's reflection, what we know would exist in a country afflicted by the extremes of poverty and wealth. If Conrad is at home with them (and was any novelist more aware of the refuse of humanity?), so much the more is he likely to be at home with the central areas of human society.

One central area of human society that Conrad exploits in *Nostromo* is the humorous. His main agent is Captain Mitchell, "a thick, elderly man, wearing high, pointed collars and short side-whiskers, partial to white waistcoats, and really very communicative under his air of pompous reserve", and one of the great comic characters in fiction. The rigid limits of his imagination gain greatly in point by being set in so wild and romantic a series of events. He is also invaluable technically as the narrator of past events when enough of these have been described directly. The chapter in which he subjects a distinguished visitor to a day's sight-seeing while his boat is in port is at once extremely funny and invaluable in disposing of a large measure of necessary action in an interesting and businesslike way. But Conrad commands also other types of humour than Captain Mitchell: gentler, for instance, and more delicate when he describes the care that Don Pépé and his friend and helper, Father Roman, take of the inhabitants of the mining villages. Don Pépé had a wonderful knowledge of them.

It was only the small fry that puzzled him sometimes. He and the padre could be seen frequently side by side, meditative and

[1] pp. 382-3.

gazing across the street of a village at a lot of sedate brown children, trying to sort them out, as it were, in low, consulting tones, or else they would together put searching questions as to the parentage of some small, staid urchin met wandering, naked and grave, along the road with a cigar in his baby mouth, and perhaps his mother's rosary, purloined for purposes of ornamentation, hanging in a loop of beads low down on his rotund little stomach.[1]

And he can be more savagely humorous, as in the description of the triumphal entry of the Monterists into Sulaco. It begins:

And first came straggling in through the land gate the armed mob of all colours, complexions, types, and states of raggedness, calling themselves the Sulaco National Guard, and commanded by Señor Gamacho. Through the middle of the street streamed, like a torrent of rubbish, a mass of straw hats, ponchos, gunbarrels, with an enormous green and yellow flag flapping in their midst, in a cloud of dust, to the furious beating of drums. The spectators recoiled against the walls of the houses shouting their *Vivas!*

The humorous element in *Nostromo* is indeed subordinate, but it is firmly there and acutely felt. It contributes substantially to the wonderful richness of the book: a richness unique in the writings of Conrad.

(iv) *Geographical Intensity*

It is the special distinction of the English novel during the nineteenth century and the first quarter of the twentieth to invest places, existent or imagined, with an air of compelling reality. Tully-Veolan in *Waverley*, the farm in *Wuthering Heights*, the marshes in *Great Expectations*, the almshouses in the *Warden*, the row of miners' cottages in *Sons and Lovers* are a few out of many examples. But for the sustained compulsion to see and believe in an imagined town and its surroundings no English novel can challenge *Nostromo*,[2] not even when its imaginings are founded on an actual place. Conrad, both in

[1] p. 102.
[2] See Appendix B for an account of the topography of Costaguana and a map of the district of Sulaco.

his introduction and in *A Personal Record*, tells us of his utter self-abandonment over nearly two years to his imagined scene and to the things that happened there. Thus living, he was oblivious of the world around him. As he himself put it:

> My sojourn on the Continent of Latin America, famed for its hospitality, lasted for about two years. On my return I found (speaking somewhat in the style of Captain Gulliver) my family all well, my wife heartily glad to learn that the fuss was all over, and our small boy considerably grown during my absence.

Of the country of Costaguana he said: "There was not a single brick, stone, or grain of sand of its soil I had not placed in position with my own hands." And the result of this utter self-dedication is that Conrad gives to his geography a most compelling sense of reality, a sense we usually confine to places known in real life over many years. It is thus that we picture the old town of Sulaco, Giorgio's house outside towards the harbour, the railway and the dusty track near it, the jetty and the Customs House, the Isabels, the mine, and ever in the background the snowy peak of Higuerota. This dedication of Conrad's self to an imagined scene makes generally for great intensity of presentation; it also denotes a heroic strain in the author. And that heroic strain generates a confidence in his ability to speak for many men.

(v) *The Tragic Theme*

(a) *Not Purely Pessimistic*

The greatest epics include within their great variety some tragic theme, some theme dealing with the fate of the individual in his struggle with circumstance and raising the issues of right and wrong. *Nostromo* resembles them through such an inclusion within its great variety. Indeed its critics have had most to say on its tragic theme and little to say on the surrounding variety; and it is true enough that this theme, rather than the variety, joins *Nostromo* to Conrad's other best work. Naturally, anyone wishing to generalise on Conrad has tended to see the things that *Nostromo* shares with its fellow-novels and to pass over the things in which it is different. But, writing of one novel, I must take all its elements (or as many as possible) into account. Thus I cannot avoid writing on the tragic theme, even though the critics have written sensibly and acutely on it already. And I am the readier to do so because, however truly they have written, some have made their truth too narrow.

This narrowing has mainly consisted of making *Nostromo* too pessimistic, of making it say at great length what Conrad has said more briefly in the *Heart of Darkness*. For instance, Leavis,[1] who has written well on the different ideals or lack of ideals of the characters, exaggerates the central and destructive doubt Conrad exhibits of the ultimate solidity of those principles of "tradition, discipline, and moral ideal" whose exemplification in concrete experience he believed in powerfully. He detects a void in the moral centre of *Nostromo*, great as that book is, a void that has its counterpart in Decoud when denied the power of action. And Hewitt[2] posits something very similar when he enlarges the scope of Conrad's 'darkness' so that it covers *Nostromo* and when he writes that, though Conrad recognises a world of moral and spiritual values, "yet every quality, every virtue, every position in which he might hope to rest in security, is at once undermined; the 'impenetrable darkness' covers the world". And he holds that Conrad had no vision of hidden good to balance his vision of hidden evil. That assertion may be true of the *Heart of Darkness*: but it is not true of *Lord Jim*, where Marlow speaks of "the Dark Powers whose real terrors, always on the verge of triumph, are perpetually foiled by the stedfastness of men"; and to apply it to *Nostromo* is, speaking symbolically, to ignore the white peak of Higuerota and to gaze only at the nocturnal darkness of the Placid Gulf. It is also a judgement which ignores several of the book's most important characters. Mrs Gould may fail in her dearest wishes, but she has been little corrupted and preserves her standards. Dr Monygham regains his self-respect. The Chief Engineer (a very important character) actually comes near to making a success of the difficult art of living. Old Viola may shoot the wrong man, but his integrity has not been destroyed.

[1] In the *Great Tradition* (London 1948), p. 192 ff.
[2] *Op. cit.*, pp. 130-1.

There is sorrow, cruelty, even despair in sufficient abundance in *Nostromo*, but they no more usurp the whole book than they do the central tragedies of Shakespeare.

Another way of narrowing Conrad's moral scope is to make much of the Conrad-Decoud resemblance, pretending that Decoud's hopeless scepticism represents Conrad's own way of presenting people and events in his novel.[1] It was Conrad who first pointed out the resemblance, and we should beware of pushing it farther than he did himself. All Conrad did was to hint that the relationship between Decoud and Antonia Avellanos had something in common with the relationship between himself when at school and a slightly older Polish girl who "was an uncompromising Puritan of patriotism". But there is the vast difference that the Polish girl's austerities were directed at the thoughtlessness of a schoolboy, Antonia's at the hollow scepticism of a man older than herself. Conrad's vision of life is broad like Homer's and Shakespeare's rather than unnaturally canalised and clarified like his Decoud's.

(b) *Corruption of the Ideal*

It is usual to centre the action of *Nostromo* on the San Tomé mine and the corruption it works in the minds of Charles Gould and of Nostromo. And that habit is correct except for not including enough. Conrad himself seems to support it by his ceaseless insistence on the silver, even to the extent of giving the Garibaldino silver-rimmed spectacles and risking an irrelevance by introducing the word into the last sentence of the book. Nevertheless, the silver of the mine not only expresses the temptation of avarice, and the pressure on the modern industrialised world of 'material interests', but represents *any* ideal to which a man gives himself and for which he works. It is only an accident that the ideal which possesses Charles Gould is attached to a mine; the same theme could have been worked out through any number of different ideals or 'causes', such as votes for women, anti-vivisection, or the collecting of Attic red-figure vases. In fact, the ruling notion of *Nostromo* is that expressed in Conrad's essay, *Autocracy and War*, that wonderful

---

[1] See Leavis, *op. cit.*, p. 199, and G. Morf, *The Polish Heritage of Joseph Conrad* (London 1930), p. 128 ff.

piece of political prescience and sagacity published in the year after the publication of *Nostromo* and in some ways the most illuminating of all comments on it. There Conrad wrote:

> It is the bitter fate of any idea to lose its royal form and power, to lose its 'virtue' the moment it descends from its solitary throne to work its will among the people.

I should hasten to add here that though this is the book's ruling notion, it is a signal error to confound all the degrees of this inevitable loss and to sink them into a common abyss of darkness. The book's intention is to present a number of these different degrees, which range from what by less austere standards could be called success to total failure.

(c) *Higuerota*

One reason why the sentence quoted is so helpful is that it points to an important truth which, to the best of my knowledge, has been missed. Transferred to the context of *Nostromo*, the phrase 'solitary throne' makes us think of the eternal snows of Higuerota; as it should do, for Higuerota is not only a most convincingly real snow-peak (as, when seen close by night from the Entrada Pass, "the white Higuerota soared out of the shadows of rock and earth like a frozen bubble under the moon") but a permanent symbol of ideal truth, sometimes forgotten but ever there in the background. It is there in its unchangingness, to judge and to set off the heroic failures, the sordid ambitions, the childish irresponsibilities, and the sickening cruelty that are manifested under its shadow. But the equation I have advanced may be doubted, and I must say something in its support.

Mentions of Higuerota, though not very many, occur so regularly that it would be strange if a deliberate purpose were not behind them. Some of them are purely descriptive, serving merely to remind the reader that the mountain has been there all the time; others have a clear symbolic purpose; others again might have one but leave you in doubt. Aptly enough the first description is of this last kind.

> On the rare clear mornings another shadow is cast upon the sweep of the gulf. The dawn breaks high behind the towering

and serrated wall of the Cordillera, a clear-cut vision of dark peaks rearing their steep slopes on a lofty pedestal of forest rising from the very edge of the shore. Amongst them the white head of Higuerota rises majestically upon the blue. Bare clusters of enormous rocks sprinkle with tiny black dots the smooth dome of snow. Then, as the midday sun withdraws from the gulf the shadow of the mountains, the clouds begin to roll out of the lower valleys. They swathe in sombre tatters the naked crags of precipices above the wooded slopes, hide the peaks, smoke in stormy trails across the snows of Higuerota.[1]

These tattered clouds darkly swathing Higuerota, are they or are they not symbolic? The answer does not matter, provided the question is asked. On the other hand, if you ask whether there is any symbolic connection between Giorgio Viola and Higuerota, the answer is a very clear *yes*. His hair is "as white as the snows of Higuerota" because his simple-minded Republican faith has not diverged too far from the original ideal on which it was founded. It is for the same reason that Viola habitually contemplated the mountain.

He had been one of the immortal and invincible band of liberators who had made the mercenaries of tyranny fly like chaff before a hurricane, "un uragano terribile". But that was before he was married and had children; and before tyranny had reared its head again amongst the traitors who had imprisoned Garibaldi, his hero. There were three doors in the front of his house, and each afternoon the Garibaldino could be seen at one or another of them with his big bush of white hair, his arms folded, his legs crossed, leaning back his leonine head against the lintel, and looking up the wooded slopes of the foothills at the snowy dome of Higuerota.

Once, and once only, Conrad gives us a close view of the mountain, and he does so partly to contrast the natures of two men, Sir John, chairman of the railway company, and the chief engineer. The scene is the Entrada Pass, where the surveying camp has been pitched. Sir John, who has "all the indifference of a man of affairs to nature, whose hostility can always be overcome by the resources of finance", arrived there "just too late to see the last dying glow of sunlight upon the

[1] p. 6.

snowy flank of Higuerota". On the other hand, the engineer-in-chief, awaiting Sir John

> at the door of a hut of rough stones, had contemplated the changing hues on the enormous side of the mountain, thinking that in this sight, as in a piece of inspired music, there could be found together the utmost delicacy of shaded expression and a stupendous magnificence of effect.

The mental gifts of the two, Conrad tells us, were "as elementally different as fire and water", and when much later in the book the engineer-in-chief says to Dr Monygham that things seem to be worth nothing by what they are in themselves: "I begin to believe that the only solid thing about them is the spiritual value which everyone discovers in his own form of activity": Conrad intends us to remember that the speaker had listened to the "inaudible strain sung by the sunset" on the snows of Higuerota, symbol of the "royal form and power" of the uncontaminated idea.

Decoud, as I have said, stands outside the fairy-tale and except on one occasion outside the influence of Higuerota. His domain is that of the intellect and the practical life. The exceptional occasion is when he bases his idea of a new state of Costaguana not only on the practical motive that only in an independent Costaguana can he win his Antonia, but on the idealistic plea that nature demands it. There is an *a priori* case for it:

> "We Occidentals have been always distinct and separated.... We have the greatest riches, the greatest fertility, the purest blood in our great families, the most laborious population. The Occidental Province should stand alone.... The rest of Costaguana hangs like a millstone round our necks. The Occidental territory is large enough to make any man's country. Look at the mountains! Nature itself seems to cry to us 'Separate!'"

And it is just because Decoud is about to announce this *a priori* reason for the separatist idea that Conrad prefaced Decoud's announcement with the words: "the night air, as if cooled by the snows of Higuerota, refreshed their faces".

Similarly the motive of Higuerota enters with the theme of Dr Monygham's disinterested devotion to Mrs Gould. "There was a great fund of loyalty in Dr Monygham's nature", and his spiritual health was wrecked when under prolonged torture he failed in his loyalty. He regained his health through directing his natural loyalty to Mrs Gould, whom he idealised. He had settled all his loyalty "on Mrs Gould's head. He believed her worthy of every devotion." And shortly after we find the sun "issuing in all the fulness of its power from behind the dazzling snow-edge of Higuerota". And when the doctor says to Mrs Gould,

> "Let me try to serve you to the whole extent of my evil reputation. I am off now to play my game of betrayal with Sotillo, and keep him off the town,"

(a game fraught with the risks of death or worse), Conrad tells us that "for a time the snows of Higuerota continued to glow with the reflected glory of the west" as "the doctor, holding a straight course for the Custom House, appeared lonely, hopping amongst the dark bushes like a tall bird with a broken wing".

(d) *The Ideal Again*

Conrad's concern with the abstracted ideal is given both beauty and weight through being centred symbolically in the single, dominant snow-peak. And that singleness and domination give point to the many varieties in the inevitable failure of human beings to live up to the ideals on which they attempt to found their conduct.

Before enlarging on samples of these, I must indicate what Conrad seems to think the besetting reason of these failures. In his preface to *Nostromo* (written of course many years after the novel) Conrad talks of his vision of a country "with its high shadowy Sierra and its misty Campo for mute witnesses of events flowing from the passions of men short-sighted in good and evil". *Nostromo* contains superb pictures of men short-sighted in evil. And at the same time it is the short sight of the well-intentioned that causes the corruption of their ideals. It is a failure of imagination. In the wonderful passage near the end of the book after Mrs Gould has been described as "a good fairy, weary with a long career of well-doing, touched by the withering suspicion of the uselessness of her labours", comes

her surmise of what it is that makes human enterprise go
wrong:

> It had come into her mind that for life to be large and full, it
> must contain the care of the past and of the future in every
> passing moment of the present. Our daily work must be done to
> the glory of the dead, and for the good of those who come after.

Whatever the full implication of these sentiments, they are at
least opposed to the error of being short-sighted in good, of
confining your good deeds to the present alone. And the only
way to knit past, present, and future together is to be infinitely
flexible and adaptable and imaginative, to know that the
premisses keep changing, not to be in love with what has ceased
to suit the changed premiss, to refrain from fondling the contours of dead experience. *Autocracy and War* contains this modi-
fying doctrine as well as the doctrine that all ideals are corrupted when put into worldly practice. There Conrad wrote:

> The sin of the old European monarchies was not the absolutism
> inherent in every form of government; it was the inability to
> alter the forms of legality, grown narrow and oppressive with
> the march of time. Every form of legality is bound to degenerate
> into oppression.

This of course puts things at their worst, but it also implies
that if a person or an institution has the imagination to change
the form of its activity to something fitting the 'march of time',
there is the hope of a better state of affairs.

To illustrate from *Nostromo* itself. It was his inability to adapt
himself that killed Charles Gould's father. He had been able
to stand the ordinary, unofficial, spasmodic extortions of individual officials in a Spanish American government, but he
could not stand official extortion in the immediate payment of
royalties on the hypothetical output of the disused mine which
had been forced on him in payment of his previous loans to the
government. Not that he was worse off than before, but he
hated the new form of the extortion, which obsessed his mind
and drove him to live within the fatal compass of the present,
forgetting Mrs Gould's moral that "for life to be large and full,
it must contain the care of the past and of the future in every
passing moment of the present". Narrowing his mind to the

single, tormenting, present issue, Gould's father sickened and died a premature death.

The terrible truth, then, that every ideal is corrupted as soon as it is translated into action is not without its mitigations. Though it allows of no exceptions, the extent of its working varies enormously, and the power of the human imagination may prevent its taking an extreme form. Conrad also allows that the humbler the ideal and the simpler the person pursuing it, the milder is the corruption involved. Captain Mitchell's ideal is practical—"We never make mistakes"—and he is a simple-minded man. And all the penalty that the translation of ideal into action exacts from Captain Mitchell is a mere mild self-deception. He flatters himself that he knows men, but has not the least idea that to the commanders of the O.S.N. Co's ships he is known as 'Fussy Joe'. And he misestimates what he owes, in the running of the port of Sulaco, to the abilities of Nostromo. Viola, the Garibaldino, also comes off lightly, on account of his great simplicity. Loyal to his hero, he cannot transfer his loyalty to a more effective place. His penalty is merely to become passive, a memory rather than a force, at best a stabilising influence on his countrymen. But morally he is uncorrupted, and the silver of the mine gets no nearer to him than to supply the frame of the spectacles through which he reads his Bible.

But the person (of all the main persons) who succeeds best in life is the engineer-in-chief of the railway. During the first half of the novel he is hardly a main person though he makes his impression. But when Decoud and Nostromo have left Sulaco harbour in the silver-laden lighter he inherits Decoud's part as critic of events and starts into prominence. He embodies what Edward Crankshaw[1] calls Conrad's "practical idealism, in spite of his own ironic pessimism", and he has the crucial virtue of adaptability. These things come out at the beginning of the third book in the conversation between the engineer and Monygham in Viola's house, after the Europeans have finished their task of loading the lighter and have dispersed, leaving the Costaguanans to settle their own conflicts. The engineer is highly intelligent and knows exactly what he is

[1] *Joseph Conrad* (London 1936), p. 19.

doing. He used his railway workers to protect property against a mob, but, that accomplished, he is not going to involve his company in politics now that the mob has been headed by the Monterists and has become political.

> Sulaco, for him, was a railway station, a terminus, workshops, a great accumulation of stores. As against the mob the railway defended its property, but politically the railway was neutral. He was a brave man; and in that spirit of neutrality he had carried proposals of truce to the self-appointed chiefs of the popular party, the deputies Fuentes and Gamacho. Bullets were still flying about when he had crossed the Plaza on that mission, waving above his head a white napkin belonging to the table linen of the Amarilla Club.

But, while faithful to the interests of the railway that employs him, he remembers those of his friends. He gives Fuentes and Gamacho the news that Pedro Montero has crossed the mountains and will be arriving at Sulaco, but by being vague about the time causes the two to ride off to meet Pedro, making it possible, for any Ribierists who wish, to escape to Los Hatos and join Hernandez. And he "thinks the railway has done pretty well by its friends without compromising itself hopelessly". As a critic of events, he shows that, while maintaining his principle of fidelity, he has the imagination to allow for the unceasing shift of the data. And he knows that such an imagination is not general. He grasps immediately the virtues of Decoud's apparently wild scheme of separatism for the province of Sulaco, saying to Monygham:

> "He had arguments which should have appeared solid enough if we, members of old, stable political and national organizations, were not startled by the mere idea of a new State evolved like this out of the head of a scoffing young man fleeing for his life, with a proclamation in his pocket, to a rough, jeering, half-bred swashbuckler, who in this part of the world is called a general. It sounds like a comic fairy tale—and behold, it may come off."

The chief engineer is thus alert: ready to consider a new idea, ever vigilant in helping men of goodwill, unsleeping in devotion to duty. He is the one main character who appears to succeed.

On the other hand, he is spared the highest responsibility, and he is lucky. He is first of all a practical man who carries out the orders of those who shape policies. He is like the captain of a ship with his set task and his duty to his owners. He may be an admirable critic, but he is spared the ultimate choice. Success for him is easier as it is limited. His luck is made apparent through his long (and for the intention of the novel) crucial conversation with Dr Monygham. And that conversation, on the present situation in Sulaco, begins and ends with a remark that takes us into the heart of Conrad's thought. As Charles Gould leaves the two together, the engineer says of him: "That man is calmness personified; he must be extremely sure of himself." To which Monygham, thinking of his own case, retorts: "If that's all he's sure of, then he is sure of nothing. It is the last thing a man should be sure of." The engineer will not have it and protests: "I really don't see that. For me there seems to be nothing else." And Dr Monygham's last word on general themes before they revert to talk about persons is: "Have you met the impossible face to face—or have you, the Napoleon of railways, no such word in your dictionary?" To which the engineer has the modesty not to reply, the fact being that he has been one of the lucky ones who has never been set an ordeal beyond his powers. Conrad believed that every man has his Achilles heel and that the Stoics were wrong in holding that the self-reliant man of virtue, the man in Horace's phrase *justus et tenax propositi*, could survive all ordeals, including the collapse of the world itself. But he also believed that some men (like Captain MacWhirr) were lucky and were subjected only to those ordeals to which they were equal. Monygham was not less courageous than the engineer-in-chief, but under prolonged torture he gave way, thereby losing his self-respect.

(e) *Congruence with Christian Doctrine*

Critics have usually seen in Conrad's admission of the Achilles heel a profound pessimism; they attribute to him a terrible belief in the darkness at the centre of every human mind, in an area of uncertainty capable at any time of confounding every noble or decent feeling or thought that exists in its other areas. And when, in his later novels, Conrad seems less obsessed with the heart of darkness, they suspect him of escapism and comparative dishonesty. But they forget that in *Nostromo* Conrad combines his theme of the heart of darkness with the other theme that in actual fact some men are not subject to its tyranny. The scene I have been discussing is an eminent example of this combination. As to pessimism, I am forced to record that *Nostromo*, taken as a whole, does not strike me as a pessimistic book. It presents too rich and exciting a picture for that and on the moral side it records a wondering bewilderment rather than expresses a certainty of the evil nature of the present world. If, of course, you are convinced that Christianity is in essence pessimistic, you will find Conrad to be so too. Otherwise you will find that his pessimism is not incompatible with the Christian scheme. Christianity has always opposed the Stoic's notion of self-sufficiency and has always held that the mind of fallen, unaided man is prone, some limited natural motions towards good apart, to fall into a state of chaos. It is Christian thought that is behind Conrad's conception of human destiny. The very prayer not to be led into temptation may be taken to imply that for every mortal some temptations are indeed too strong. And when Conrad both admits this and records that in actual fact some men seem to survive their ordeals, he is not straying from the religion in which he was brought up. And if thereafter he does nothing more definite than recognise and present a mystery, can more be expected of him as an artist or can it be said that Shakespeare did otherwise? On the contrary, in its richness and its mystery Conrad's presentation of the human predicament reminds me of Shakespeare's most of all.

(vi) *The Tragic Heroes*

So far I have said little about Charles Gould and Gian Battista Fidanza or Nostromo, the two chief victims of the San Tomé mine. And in so doing I have not meant to imply that their fates are not, nominally at least, the master themes of the book. I say nominally, because there is something false in the great prominence given to Nostromo. This qualification does not apply to Gould. He is indeed the tragic hero, whose wife's fate is tied up with his; and Nostromo, contrasted with Gould both in his character and in the way the silver works on it, is his most effective foil.

Critics have concentrated mainly on the evil that the mine works in Gould, as they have exaggerated the pessimism of the whole book, and have missed the poignancy engendered by the amount of good in him and in his acts, good which is yet unable to keep him straight. They have also tended to put Gould's errors in terms of 'material interests' solely and to omit the partial but most important additional error of inflexibility. Conrad himself may have been partly responsible. While the course of the story plainly indicates that Gould erred for more than one reason, Conrad himself, by his own statements or implications, presses the 'silver' theme from a very early stage, even taking it back to the time when the mine was predominantly a power for good. One of Conrad's tiresome habits is to overdo the theme or the symbol iterated for the sake of the construction. He overdoes the darkness theme in the *Heart of Darkness* and the youth theme in *Youth*. And in *Nostromo* he does the same with silver and 'material interests'. I incline therefore to write off some of Conrad's implications, when they are the fruit of his craftsman's conscience, and to rely more on what his story tells us. And what it tells us about Gould is not that his idealist experiment with the mine was a mistake, doomed from the beginning, but that it involved a great risk, which only consummate self-knowledge and adaptability could be safe from. Up to a point Gould, with his wife's help, succeeded. The patriarchical working of the mine suited the native Costaguanan and won his heart. Justice prevailed beyond the bridge which separated the San Tomé kingdom from every alien intrusion; justice such as had never been known there since the mine was first worked. And the practical expression of the genuine response that Gould's integrity and devotion called forth was the spontaneous movement of the workers to march in a body with what arms they could collect to rescue their chief from the Monterist revolutionaries. And not the men alone. Captain Mitchell actually touches eloquence as he describes the strange scene (and note that his description of these folk of goodwill on the march is made to echo the comic account, quoted above, of the rascally Monterists pouring into Sulaco).

> "A terrible fire, by the light of which I saw the last of the fighting, the llaneros flying, the Nationals throwing their arms down, and the miners of San Tomé, all Indians from the Sierra, rolling by like a torrent to the sound of pipes and cymbals, green flags flying, a wild mass of men in white ponchos and green hats, on foot, on mules, on donkeys. Such a sight, sir, will never be seen again. The miners, sir, had marched upon the town, Don Pépé leading on his black horse, and their very wives in the rear on burros, screaming encouragement, sir, and beating tambourines. I remember one of these women had a green parrot seated on her shoulder, as calm as a bird of stone. They had just saved their Señor Administrador."

Only if one does full justice to the nobility of these feelings of spontaneous gratitude and devotion and to the noble qualities in the Goulds that evoked them can one appreciate the full tragedy of the sequel when the mine loses its personal basis and becomes a soulless machine turning out more and more wealth and dehumanising those who work it; only thus can one see the full import of Dr Monygham's ruthless remark to Mrs Gould:

> "Do you think that now the mine would march upon the town to save their Señor Administrador? Do you think that?"

Part of Gould's crime, then, was that he could not foresee the change if he allowed the mine to go on expanding; he is guilty of fondling the contours of dead experience; dead now, even if once alive and lovely.

Of course, I am not denying the cruder form of corruption that works on Gould and of which his wife has not the least taint. Both rejoice in the steadying effect the mine has on the province of Sulaco:

> For them both, each passing of the escort under the balconies of the Casa Gould was like another victory gained in the conquest of peace for Sulaco.

Yet Charles Gould, even in the fairly early days, "told his wife once *with some exultation*, there had never been seen anything in the world to approach the vein of the Gould Concession". And that exultation was coarse, dangerous, and very different from that of his wife's when she

> laid her unmercenary hands, with an eagerness that made them tremble, upon the first silver ingot turned out still warm from the mould; and by her imaginative estimate of its power she endowed that lump of metal with a justificative conception, as though it were not a mere fact, but something far-reaching and impalpable, like the true expression of an emotion or the emergence of a principle.

The mixture in the reasons for Gould's enslavement to the mine come out perfectly in Mrs Gould's mental soliloquy near the end of the book after her long talk with Dr Monygham in which occurs his cruel insistence that the miners would not now march to rescue their manager and after the description of her as the good fairy baffled in her beneficence. She sees her husband as incorrigible, incorrigible in his devotion to the mine, in his "hard determined service of the material interests to which he had pinned his faith in the triumph of order and justice". The success of the mine had been colossal. But "there was something inherent in the necessities of successful action which carried with it the moral degradation of the idea". But he could not see it, and she, cut off, could not tell him. The reasons are all there: the inflexibility of mind, the yielding to the attractions of wealth and sheer size, the preference for the ease of actions narcotic before the rigour of reflection. And yet Gould is a perfect Aristotelian hero, capable of great heroism and nobility, more good than bad, brought down by failure in a part of his nature. As such he provides a centre for the novel and vastly raises it in strength, dignity, and pathos.

As a foil to Charles Gould, Nostromo quite fulfils his function. He is also an astonishingly successful character-creation. We accept him completely, yet he stands neat and clear from all other feigned characters. And this clarity together with the good things critics have already said of him as a foil to Charles Gould make it superfluous for me to say more about him in general. On the other hand it was mainly through the way

Conrad developed the story and the character of Nostromo that he fell into certain faults which have been described in part but whose extent has not yet been seen and faced. So this seems the right place to discuss these.

(vii) *Faults*

Crankshaw[1] saw that the direct account of Nostromo's state of mind when alone in the darkness after leaving Decoud is not up to standard, and that it would have been better if Nostromo could have reappeared suddenly in Sulaco and then "later, in his own words, in his confession to Giselle perhaps, have recalled the substance of his revelations hanging between life and death". Crankshaw notes that the account of Decoud's suicide also is not up to standard. This picture of his state of mind is somewhat lurid; we know enough already of him to be able to guess at his motives; and the bare hints given by the deserted island, the missing pieces of silver, and the empty boat could have spoken more effectively. With all this I agree; but Crankshaw does not go far enough, for there is something specious about Conrad's whole development of Nostromo's enslavement to the silver and especially about the two last chapters recounting his entanglement with Giselle and his death.

Such an assertion may seem rash when you think of the closeness with which the last episodes are integrated with the rest; but we should bear Hewitt's comment on Conrad's method in mind:

> Such a method assures great coherence and concentration and the possibility of a powerful expression of the states of mind of his characters. But clearly it could be used to give force to themes which were at bottom trivial, melodramatic or sentimental.[2]

The last sentence indicates perfectly the faults of these episodes. True, you could defend the last pages because they contain one of the great moments of the novel: when Mrs Gould reproves Giselle's more superficial despair with the words, "I have been loved too." But one great moment cannot redeem

[1] *Op. cit.*, pp. 157-8.　　　　[2] *Op. cit.*, pp. 14-15.

two whole chapters. To come to some of the points where Conrad deteriorates, he fails not only in describing directly Nostromo's lonely feelings on board the lighter (as Crankshaw noted) but, later, in describing the same man's feelings when, after jumping from Barrios's steamer, he has boarded the empty drifting boat. Thus far Conrad has led up skilfully to the change in Nostromo's state of mind that causes him to steal the silver and he has done so by hints. But now, when it comes to the turning-point, to the possession of Nostromo's body by an alien soul, he grows artificial and, instead of just writing his account, writes it up. Conrad has already told us that the "Capataz of the Sulaco Cargadores resembled a drowned corpse come up from the bottom to idle away the sunset hour in a small boat". And he shortly gives this paragraph to describe how that corpse was occupied by an intruder:

> And now, with the means of gaining the great Isabel thrown thus in his way at the earliest possible moment, his excitement had departed, as when the soul takes flight leaving the body inert upon an earth it knows no more. Nostromo did not seem to know the gulf. For a long time even his eyelids did not flutter once upon the glazed emptiness of his stare. Then slowly, without a limb having stirred, without a twitch of muscle or quiver of an eyelash, an expression, a living expression came upon the still features, deep thought crept into the empty stare—as if an outcast soul, a quiet, brooding soul, finding that untenanted body in its way, had come in stealthily to take possession.[1]

This is eloquent, but it is very solemn. And it is not at all appropriate to that flamboyance of Nostromo's character which disperses instantaneously every hint of solemnity. Conrad, I fear, is faking. Then, in the love-passages between Nostromo and Giselle there is some very poor writing:

> She listened as if in a trance. Her fingers stirred in his hair. He got up from his knees reeling, weak, empty, as though he had flung his soul away.

> Her smooth forehead had the pure, soft sheen of a priceless pearl in the splendour of the sunset, mingling the gloom of starry spaces, the purple of the sea, and the crimson of the sky in a magnificent stillness.

[1] p. 493.

The magnificent Capataz clasped her round her white neck in
the darkness of the gulf as a drowning man clutches at a straw.

The first and third passages are trite; the second is pretentious
but fails to create a credible picture, indeed to achieve any
result. As a last example of inferior quality, I take the famous
ending. It will not bear examination. Conrad asserts that
Linda's cry of undying fidelity "was another of Nostromo's
triumphs, the greatest, the most enviable, the most sinister of
all". Can he really believe that? was it a triumph at all for
Nostromo to have won the heart of a not especially attractive,
extremely possessive girl, deprived of all eligible male society,
who had been nurtured on the idea of his being a hero from a
very early age? And the "conquests of treasure and love", the
words which end the book, cost Nostromo small effort, compared with a dozen of his other feats; they simply do not merit
the supremely prominent place they are given.

It is easy to see why Conrad thus went wrong at the end. His
case is that of the bird that has failed to shed all the shell of the
egg out of which it was hatched. A story of silver stolen by a
sailor engendered the whole complexity of the novel, including
themes more weighty than itself. But Conrad was loyal to his
engendering episode and pitted it against something bigger:
Gould's involvement in his inherited mine and great political
issues. Having disposed of his greater themes, he was led
unconsciously and unnaturally to inflate the smaller one. Instead of tying it in to the greater in decent subordination, he
must needs isolate and continue it. Thus isolated it reveals its
weakness, and Conrad vainly tried to put things right by
inflating it beyond its natural and legitimate dimensions.

However, these faults are not more than rather serious
faults of detail; they do not endanger the main constructions
or compromise the authentic wealth and variety of content
found everywhere else.

(viii) *The Construction*

Critics of *Nostromo* are agreed that Conrad controlled and
shaped his matter with conspicuous success. Still, having

underestimated the extent and variety of that matter, they have thereby underestimated the difficulty of the task to which he was committed. And so let it be said that in *Nostromo* Conrad does indeed show a control commensurate with the amount he includes and that he gets as near the structural ideal as a man is likely to get: the ideal that the whole, however long, should remain fluid and unset till the last word has been written, that the writer should have everything simultaneously in mind and keep all the parts open to modification throughout the process of composition. It was his complete self-dedication to his task, his act of living for two years in feigned Costaguana instead of in the real world around him, that made his success possible.

I come now to the construction; and here it is easier to accumulate evidence for an uncommon closeness of interlocking through the great abundance of cross-references than it is to say how Conrad succeeds in the general control and disposition of his material. This is an affair of proportion; and at least I can say that he got right the proportions of central tragedy and enriching episode and circumstance, of stirring action and the reflection needed to give that action a meaning. Charles Gould is like the soloist in a well-balanced concerto. He stands out, he attracts notice; but not at the expense of the richness of the orchestral background. The action is very full, interesting in itself, and contains all the elements of surprise and suspense required to make it self-sufficient as a mere unpondered sequence of events. If Conrad had maintained the ordinary time sequence, the bare action might have run away with him and prevented his saying through it the things he wanted to say. By ranging backwards and forwards in the sequence he avoids the danger and succeeds in charging action with meaning without destroying its interest as a sequence. I have already mentioned one master-stroke: that of using Captain Mitchell as the narrator of a very substantial piece of past history. Not only was it necessary to summarise at this place, the crowd of events being too great to admit of fully developed narration except at the price of tedium, spiritual redundance, and excessive length, but the complete change of climate caused by the humour of Mitchell's pomposities refreshes and reinvigorates the reader. As artist, Conrad in *Nostromo* has just that tact and adaptability whose lack in the affairs of life he shows to be a principal reason why his imagined characters get into trouble.

Critics have noted many of the repetitions, cross-references, and contrasts that tie the parts of the book together. And they will find many more over the years, for every fresh reading discovers examples not noticed before. I have already touched on some of these incidentally, for instance the repetitions of the fairy theme and of Higuerota, and the way Captain Mitchell's account of the miners invading Sulaco echoes the account of the Monterist rabble doing the same. Here are a couple more examples of what happens constantly. After Decoud has enlarged on the theme of the English invading and exploiting Spanish America, Conrad refers back to it by describing the great Sala of the Casa Gould "with its groups of ancient Spanish and modern European furniture making as if different centres". Dr Monygham, about to deceive Sotillo concerning the hiding-place of the silver in order to keep him busy in the harbour where he will not threaten Charles Gould's safety, says to Mrs Gould, "Let me try to serve you to the whole extent of my evil reputation." He is thereby contrasted simultaneously, first with Charles Gould, who refuses to go to the whole extent of his initial methods of bribery (methods in themselves an evil but justified, according to Gould, for the end's sake) by which alone the mine can be worked, and second with Nostromo, who is about to betray his own enormous good reputation and serve himself alone by stealing the silver. Such cross-references give pleasure in themselves, stimulate the mind to be on the watch for others, and draw together the different parts of the work.

Besides the main proportions and the small cross-references there are intermediate contrasts, of which the following is a sufficient sample. The account of the two Goulds in the first months after their arrival in Costaguana surveying the country in company with Don Pépé is one of lyrical beauty. It befits the mood of the newly married couple and the beauty of the untouched countryside when the San Tomé gorge is still, in Don Pépé's words, a "paradise of snakes". There is nothing to match it later in the book. There are superb descriptions, but none of this lyrical kind. But Conrad both keeps alive our memory of his description and asserts its present irrelevance by his mentions of its sole-remaining memorial: the water-colour Mrs Gould painted of the gorge while its stream still flowed in natural freedom and before it was diverted to make water-power. The very fragility of the medium used for the sketch is greatly to the point.

In those two years of composition Conrad seems to have been in a continuous mood of creative excitement and to have applied his conscious will simultaneously to an eminent degree. He achieved the kind of ordering that we expect in the most closely constructed epics in verse.

(ix) *Politics*

(a) *General*

Miss Bradbrook[1] wrote in 1941, "Whatever else in Conrad has dated, his politics are contemporary." And again, "Conrad's political writings are few, but almost without exception they are apt to the present time." The general sentiment is as true today as in 1941; Conrad's politics are frighteningly real: but his political writings bulk larger than Miss Bradbrook allows. *Nostromo*, though so much else, is a political novel, and, as such, ampler and of a deeper wisdom than the *Secret Agent* and *Under Western Eyes*. It is the essay, *Autocracy and War*, that best points to *Nostromo's* political content. It was provoked by the Russo-Japanese War and was published in 1905; and it contains not only a grim onslaught on Tsarist Russia (corresponding to the political doctrine of *Under Western Eyes* and the satire on revolutionaries in the *Secret Agent*) but a survey (highly simplified and personal of course) of political currents in western Europe throughout the nineteenth century. The political doctrine implicit in *Nostromo* is exactly that of the survey in *Autocracy and War*, extending even to such a detail as the common use of the phrase 'material interests'.

There is no cause for surprise. The Poland Conrad was

[1] M. C. Bradbrook, *Joseph Conrad* (Cambridge 1941), pp. 8-9.

brought up in was seething with political passions. He had revisited it in 1903 and that visit reawakened his own political feelings and probably inspired his political novels. He recorded that Antonia Avellanos was modelled on a Polish girl-patriot, and something of Poland has got into Costaguana. I cannot accept the close parallel that Morf[1] has perceived, but I am sure that Poland, by the mere act of bringing Conrad's political feelings and beliefs and forecasts to the boil, had a decisive effect on the temper of *Nostromo*. There is plenty of evidence that Conrad thought steadily and eagerly on politics and history as soon as he reached an age of reflection. For instance, F. M. Ford[2] wrote that he was "above all things else a politician" and that he was "a student of politics, without prescription, without dogma, and, as a Papist, with a profound disbelief in the perfectibility of human institutions". Again, Conrad wrote to Curle[3] of his interest even in party politics as well as in "the development of institutions and opinions" and added that "I feel deeply what happens in the world—a genuine sentiment qualified by irony". Conrad also wrote of his hatred of political cocksureness, of "the calm assurance of revolutionaries". Curle bears witness to Conrad's knowledge of European affairs and to his political sagacity in international politics:

> His knowledge of European affairs for hundreds of years back was encyclopaedic. . . . He had a grasp of national characteristics which made him apprehend to an almost prophetic degree the mistakes that countries made in dealing with one another.

(b) *In 'Autocracy and War'*

Having said so much about Conrad's general preoccupations with politics, and before writing of the politics of *Nostromo*, I will say more about *Autocracy and War* both to make my remarks more plausible and because this remarkable essay has had little attention. Conrad wrote his essay in an England which was just working up for the Liberal triumph of 1906,

[1] *Op. cit.*, pp. 143-6, where he equates, for instance, Sulaco with Cracow, and Garibaldi with Kosciuszko.

[2] *Joseph Conrad, a Personal Reminiscence* (London 1924), p. 58.

[3] See Richard Curle, *The Last Twelve Years of Joseph Conrad* (London 1938), pp. 26, 35-6.

which was quite pervaded by optimistic beliefs in progress, and which put progress in the simplest terms of economic and social improvement. It was an England that was profoundly unaware of 1914 and its various consequences. Conrad, deeply moved by Japan's having dissipated the illusion of Russia's invincibility, considers the consequences in the light of his assessment of European history in the nineteenth century. That assessment concentrates mainly on two matters. First, Conrad notes a spiritual deterioration in international affairs during the century. Before Sadowa and Sedan there was such an entity as Europe; there was a kind of bond, the engenderer of certain decencies, between the old dynastic monarchies. But from 1870 a new thoroughness of hate entered warfare. Second, Conrad notes that democracy fell a victim to "the incredible infatuation which could put its trust in the peaceful nature of industrial and commercial competition". The nature of this competition is active and aggressive. Nations committed to it as a main end must precipitate wars:

> The idea of ceasing to grow in territory, in strength, in wealth, in influence—in anything but wisdom and self-knowledge—is odious to them as the omen of the end. . . . Let us act lest we perish—is the cry. And the only form of action open to a state can be of no other than aggressive nature.

Once war was a thing men prayed should be averted, a plague like other plagues. Now it has been brought away from its distant home and become domesticated. Men, "after clinging for ages to the steps of the heavenly throne are now trying to steal the thunderbolts of Jupiter; they have dragged the scourge down from the skies and have made it into a calm and regulated institution". Such a sham can only lead to more and bitterer wars in the future. It was an error to associate wars only with the ambitions of the old monarchies, for there will be more and worse wars in the future:

> The era of wars so eloquently denounced by the old Republicans as the peculiar blood guilt of dynastic ambitions is by no means over yet. They will be fought out differently, with lesser frequency, with an increased bitterness and the savage tooth-and-claw obstinacy of a struggle for existence. They will make us regret the time of dynastic ambitions, with their human absurdity

moderated by prudence and even by shame, by the fear of personal responsibility and the regard paid to certain forms of conventional decency.

As for the immediate future, the first effect of the Russo-Japanese war is to encourage Germany to aggressive expansion. Her only aim and ideal consists in the "expansion of material interests" and she is supremely dangerous.

The German eagle with a Prussian head looks all round the horizon, not so much for something to do that would count for good in the records of the earth, as simply for something good to eat. He gazes upon the land and upon the sea with the same covetous steadiness.

The prophetic truth of all these remarks is too obvious to need insisting on; and the truth, except for a change in the position of Germany, extends right to the present hour. What is so remarkable is that Conrad should have foreseen so much while domiciled in the blindness of England of 1905.

But Conrad is not entirely pessimistic. He glances at the faint possibility of countries agreeing on spheres of commercial interest, an agreement that might be a temporary expedient for keeping the peace. More important (and perhaps more prophetic) is his belief that the old European monarchies, though decaying, were justified historically through their transcendence of a purely national principle.

This service of unification, creating close-knit communities possessing the ability, the will, and the power to pursue a common ideal, has prepared the ground for the advent of a still larger understanding: for the solidarity of Europeanism, which must be the next step towards the advent of Concord and Justice; an advent that, however delayed by the fatal worship of force and the errors of national selfishness, has been, and remains, the only possible goal of our progress.

Thus, though the old Europe was destroyed in 1870 and cannot be revived, it contained the germ of the United Europe of the future. Though Conrad is certain that this should be the immediate aim, he is not at all certain in his expectations that the "fatal worship of force and the errors of national selfishness" will be overcome. True, as well as the possibility of war being postponed through an agreement about zones of material interests, there is the hope that for a little the "fear of wounds" may be stronger than the "pinch of hunger": a hope that has been reinforced in our own day through immensely increased powers of wounding. But the prospect of discarding the worship of force and of erecting the true temple of peace is distant: "the very ground for its erection has not been cleared of the jungle". On the other hand, Conrad is not certain that it *won't* be erected. A turn away from action and material interests and towards reflection and intelligence is not out of the question.

Such is the doctrine of *Autocracy and War*, and permeating the essay, though not stated directly, is Conrad's own belief in the ideals of concord and justice.

I have cited the doctrines of *Autocracy and War* because they duplicate closely, even to details, the political doctrine of *Nostromo* and thus confirm my conviction, arrived at merely from reading the novel and before I had read the essay, that *Nostromo*, besides being much else, is a political novel about western Europe and that the picture of Spanish America, however fascinating and plausible, is subordinated morally to a greater political theme. It is worth mentioning a couple more of these duplicating details (the common use of the key-phrase 'material interests' has already been noted). Giorgio Viola, the Garibaldino, with his simple and noble republicanism now out of date, duplicates the 'old Republicans' of *Autocracy and War* who erroneously confined the guilt of making wars to dynastic ambitions. The rifles that Decoud introduced into Sulaco, outmoded in Europe but of the latest pattern for South America, duplicate this mention in the essay:

> There are many kinds of aggressions, though the sanction of them is one and the same—the magazine rifle of the latest pattern.

Conrad's steady belief in abstract values that permeates the essay is duplicated by the symbol of Higuerota in the novel. All these details, to which others could be added, serve to prove that novel and essay issued from the same phase of Conrad's thinking.

(c) *In 'Nostromo'*

Coming to the politics of *Nostromo*, I must remind the reader that I have touched on some of them already in pointing to its historical content. Conrad made Sulaco an antique and aristocratic province because he wanted to include in his scope the change from a feudal and personal polity to an industrialised and socialised one. Similarly, the history of the San Tomé mine from a paternal affair owned, worked, and completely known by one man to its transformation into the San Tomé Consolidated Mines Limited with its quite serious labour troubles is the symbol of what happened in western Europe during the nineteenth century. The Garibaldino, superannuated, telling his tales of the past or looking at Higuerota but irrelevant to the present happenings in Sulaco, represents the disappointment of the early, disinterested Republicans, who believed that purer governments would succeed the wreck of the old corrupt monarchies and who never suspected that democracy would ally itself to 'material interests'. Nostromo again is not only a superbly realised character in his own right but the embodiment of political facts. He is the man of the people, energetic, resourceful, but unable to direct himself: hence the predestined victim of the plans of others. And one could expose many more political facts from the substance of the novel.

But it is not the facts but the moral that matters most. And the central piece of political morality is the San Tomé mine. This, as well as being responsible for the personal tragedies of Gould and Nostromo, is the symbol of the perverted political doctrine: *First seek ye material interests and the Kingdom of God shall be added unto you*. Gould's error in thinking that the mine could be the pure instrument of good is also the enormous error of the whole western world in thinking that 'progress', the road to the millennium, lies first through economic betterment. Conrad in fact expresses a very simple thing, the present profound distrust in the ultimate benefits of material and scientific progress, the suspicion that the element of action has hopelessly preponderated over the element of thought, that man has become the slave of his own inventions. These thoughts are profoundly commonplace, nor were they new even in Conrad's own day. But he felt them in his own pulses and did not borrow them from others, and he gave them an artistic form far more lovely and compelling than any other English writer has done. Moreover, he has lasted into an age when a great body of opinion ratifies his belief and of whom (perhaps at the moment more potentially than in fact) he is the mouthpiece. Ruskin and Samuel Butler shared some of Conrad's root doctrines, but they do not speak for us today as Conrad does in *Nostromo*, which is choric in the way a true epic must be.

There is one big difference between *Autocracy and War* and *Nostromo*. The essay puts 'material interests' in vaguely European terms, but with special reference to Germany; the novel puts them mainly in terms of England and America. Through Gould Conrad expressed both his great admiration for the English character and his tragic sense of the materialism to which it had become subservient. About America he is less tragic and more humorously satirical. His American devotees of material interests are a good deal more simple-minded than Gould. First, there are the legendary Americanos, deluded by legends of gold on Azuera and coming to grief there. Then there is Mrs Gould's puzzlement at the unthinking activity of the race, typified by the three American business men (Holroyd among them) who visited the Casa Gould.

"My dear Charley, I heard those men talk among themselves. Can it be that they really wish to become, for an immense consideration, drawers of water and hewers of wood to all the countries and nations of the earth? It seemed to me that Mr Holroyd looked on his own God as a sort of influential partner, who gets his share of profits in the endowment of churches. That's a sort of idolatry. He told me endowed churches every year, Charley."

And, lastly, there is Holroyd's own declaration of his country's policy:

Now, what is Costaguana? It is the bottomless pit of 10 per cent. loans and other fool investments. European capital has been flung into it with both hands for years. Not ours, though. We in this country know just about enough to keep indoors when it rains. We can sit and watch. Of course, some day we shall step in. We are bound to. But there's no hurry. Time itself has got to wait on the greatest country in the whole of God's universe. We shall be giving the word for everything: industry, trade, law, journalism, art, politics, and religion, from Cape Horn clear over to Smith's Sound, and beyond, too, if anything worth taking hold of turns up at the North Pole. And then we shall have the leisure to take in hand the outlying islands and continents of the earth. We shall run the world's business whether the world likes it or not. The world can't help it—and neither can we, I guess.

There, in its crudest form, is the doctrine of first seeking material interests and then being sure of the other things. Conrad was not unfair. The simple-minded faith in the certain benefits of material progress, however fiercely repudiated by a minority, still prevails more in America than in the countries of western Europe.

(x) *Epic Quality*

Nostromo may thus be extremely appropriate to our present opinions, yet in one way it differs radically from anything that is being written now; and that is in the serene security of Conrad's belief in his ideals. He can talk of Justice and Concord without affectation and sentimentality and with great conviction. Men may err through acting precipitately and being too lazy to think, but Conrad is perfectly certain that if they did think more they would do better. Thus, though there is much in *Nostromo* that is frightening and on the face of it pessimistic, the net effect of its politics and its morals is strangely exhilarating. It makes you want to share in life not less but more vigorously; and that is just what most modern fiction fails to do. It thus corresponds to the wishes of a great body of people today; it echoes and confirms the hopes of those who wish to have reasons for living vigorously in a world that threatens to baffle them at every turn. Thus *Nostromo* fulfils the choric task that belongs properly to the epic.

Speaking of Conrad and Yeats, Miss Bradbrook[1] observed that "both deserve the epithet *majestic*; their power to write of the great simple heroic themes almost frightens the modern reader". And this sentiment confirms my experience of constantly thinking of Homer when reading *Nostromo*; an experience that I do not in the least have when reading the work published eighteen years later which was deliberately constructed on the pattern of the *Odyssey* and which I shall shortly go on to consider. Conrad's treatment of the great themes of action and reflection, of material interests and moral idealism, recalls the Homeric theme in the *Iliad* of the irreconcilable virtues of heroic valour and the ordered domestic life. Conrad's union of colour and romance and fairy-lore with irony and the most accurate eye for the living detail recalls Homer's union of the fabulous with the actual in the *Odyssey*. And they are alike in the span of life they cover and in the sense of teeming life within that span. This spontaneous comparison of *Nostromo* with Homer suggests that in this one book Conrad achieved an epic in the medium of prose fiction: a suggestion confirmed by the control Conrad maintained over his multifarious material and the force of later opinion of which he has become the mouthpiece.

I have no doubt of the greatness of *Nostromo*, but I am uncertain of the degree of greatness and on this point I question if anyone can at present have a firm opinion. So much depends on how the style of the book wears. In the course of time will its colour become a little quaint, will what now attracts and dazzles degenerate a little into the charm of a period piece? That is possible, and yet I do not think it likely; and my hope is that *Nostromo* (some weaknesses apart) will gradually emerge from the ordinary level of high quality into one of the great books of world literature.

[1] *Op. cit.*, p. 7.

7

Middlemarch and Bursley

(i) 'Middlemarch'

IN my *English Epic and its Background*, published in 1954, I asserted that "George Eliot in *Middlemarch* was able to get nearer to the epic than any other of the great Victorian novelists". My last reading of Arnold Bennett's *Old Wives' Tale* had been some years earlier; and though I had then admired and enjoyed it I conjectured from memory that it was too thinly written, the work of evidently too small a man, to attain anywhere near the stature of epic. More recent reading and reflection have forced me to change both these opinions.

Middlemarch remains decidedly the greater work. But its qualities are not of the epic kind. I had thought that it might be choric in two ways: in interpreting first the 'accepted unconscious metaphysic' of an English provincial area and second the aspirations of many women for a less confined life. But Middlemarch and the surrounding country reveal no metaphysic: they are admirably portrayed, but they remain setting. The book is not about Middlemarch, but about people who happen to live in and around it. Of all the characters only Caleb Garth bears a metaphysic; that of disinterested creation through toil. But as borne by him it is painfully obvious and correspondingly ineffective. Of all the larger characters, Caleb Garth is the least alive, the least productive of warmth in the reader. To seek affinity with the epic through him would be ludicrous. As to the feminism, you can point to the last pages and by careful abstraction of sentences show that George Eliot, like many others, deplored the restrictions that still hampered the scope of the intelligent, the active, the idealist members of the female sex. But, over the whole passage, she shows herself tolerably resigned to them. She does not expect for her Dorothea the clear and emphatic scope of an Antigone or a Teresa, nor does she minimise the sum of what

Dorothea achieved through all the hidden and divided chan-
nels of her activity. And if from these last pages, so emphatic
by their position, so curiously explicit compared with almost
all that have preceded, we derive no belief that George Eliot
was speaking for aspiring womanhood, we are most unlikely
to derive such a belief from the rest of the book.

Middlemarch, in spite of its length, its wealth of characters,
its leisurely unfolding of an ample setting, deals, not with a
group, but with individuals. The predicaments, tragi-comic
and tragic, of two people, Dorothea and Lydgate, dominate
and characterise the novel. And if any further refutation of a
feminist theme is wanted, you have only to reflect that Lydgate, the male with the utmost personal scope and wealth of
choice, suffers a worse thwarting than Dorothea with all her
initial confinement. How simple, had George Eliot wished to
put the feminism first, for her to have devised a very different
sort of contrast.

Middlemarch is a novel of personal relations; and its morality
has to do with the individual choice.

(ii) *The Clayhanger Trilogy*

Through the coherence of its plot and the sustention of its
style the *Old Wives' Tale* is raised well above the rest of Bennett's
more serious works. Yet some of those other works can serve
just as well to show to what literary kind he inclines and,
incidentally, to contrast this inclination with that of George
Eliot. The Clayhanger Trilogy, his next serious work in time
and importance after the *Old Wives' Tale*, is a loose chronicle,
not a tight organism, and contains poor as well as good writing.
But it is about Bursley and the other Five Towns more than
Middlemarch is about the place which supplied its title, while
the characters are more attached to their surroundings, sometimes even enslaved by them. Edwin Clayhanger, wanting to
be an architect, puts up little resistance to his father, who,
conditioned by Bursley, will have none of it; and the incident
is more about the provincial conservatism of Bursley than
about the spiritual revolt of the individual, Edwin Clayhanger.
Or take George Eliot's failure with Garth (and with types of

virtuous workmen in her other novels) and Arnold Bennett's success with James Yarlett ("Big James"), foreman of the Clayhanger printing establishment. Not only is Big James, with his impressive bulk, his great bass voice, his slight but gentle pomposity, his bachelordom, and his lack of ambition, perfectly satisfying and credible as a character, but he embodies the deep belief in solid and unskimped work that was part of the authentic creed of the Five Towns. Unlike Garth, he never appears to preach the creed, he merely enacts and embodies it.

Again, take possibly the greatest single episode in the Clayhanger Trilogy, the Sunday School Centenary in the first of the series. It does not lack touches of individual feeling or pathos: for instance, the plight of the aged and drivelling Mr Shushions (in his youth the rescuer of Darius Clayhanger from the workhouse and the founder of his fortune). He had lost his ticket, was in consequence kept away from the platform, where he belonged, and was baited by the crowd. It is a memorable episode. Memorable too is the range of passions that comprises the animal-like crudity of the crowd and the tenderness of Hilda Lessways towards its victim. But such things are subordinated to the depiction of group feeling. The Centenary was tasteless, muddled, and exhausting. But it compelled. The organisers and participants did not know what it was really about, what meaning it had for *them*, but they knew that it had power and that it meant something. Even those to whom it was most distasteful could not resist its compulsion in the end; they were drawn out of their homes to watch the show. Through this episode Bennett expresses the accepted and yet unconscious metaphysic of a group; he has created an epic fragment. This does not mean that the Clayhanger Trilogy is epic; on the contrary the episode of the Centenary is exceptional in its epic quality: and the trilogy mainly informs and describes without interpreting. It is also spun out and repetitive: it tires us with its insistence on the effect of time, the degradation of disease, and the wonder of the quotidian. Nevertheless, if it had been a better work of art, the betterment would have been in an epic and not some other direction.

The Clayhanger Trilogy and *Middlemarch* are thus sharply

opposed through their inclinations towards and away from the epic; and this contrast is not unlike that already noted between *Robinson Crusoe* and *Tom Jones*. *Tom Jones*, like *Middlemarch*, is about people, even if, unlike *Middlemarch*, it presents them in a purely comic light: and both delight by the amplitude, brilliance, and charm of the setting in which the people are placed. *Robinson Crusoe* and the Clayhanger Trilogy are immeasurably different on the surface, and a good deal different beneath it. But they unite in interpreting communal feeling, and their setting is not setting merely. Their orientation (as distinct from their success in arrival) is towards epic.

(iii) *The 'Old Wives' Tale'*

(a) *Its Competence*

Arnold Bennett still has his readers, but, I conjecture, almost entirely from the over-fifties of the population. To a younger generation his undisturbed realism, his shameless obviousness, and his habits of repetition are annoying. Perhaps it may help to counteract such annoyance if I state that I am as surprised as they could be that the *Old Wives' Tale* insisted after all in getting an honourable place in this volume. I had admired it in earlier readings but felt sure that a re-reading in the light of more literary experience and under the pressure of changing taste would show the book up as inferior; ambitious in scope but too poor in style to validate its ambitions. Having begun re-reading with the Clayhanger Trilogy and having found this good only in patches, I was confirmed in my expectations and thought it was barely worth while to turn to the *Old Wives' Tale*. Still, I did turn to it and found that it belonged to a different order of art from the Clayhanger Trilogy.[1]

First, it is, stylistically, all of a piece. Not that the style is uncharacteristic of Bennett. It is his proper style, but intensified and sustained. It does its job as cleanly and as strongly in the last twenty pages as anywhere in the book. Bennett,

[1] Bennett spent five or six years meditating on the *Old Wives' Tale* before beginning to write. See Reginald Pound, *Arnold Bennett* (London 1952), p. 180.

plainly, gave himself more completely to his imagined world than he ever did before and after. It is not that he displayed unexpected resources of his imagination, becoming for the moment a different person. Rather it is that he was his best self and his whole self all the time. His proper light burnt with an added clarity; his senses were just a little more alive than usual. Such clarity and life do not lead to striking phrases and large surprises but to numberless quiet but effective observations. Here is an example. Constance and Sophia Baines are talking delightedly in the shop to Gerald Scales, who has made a surprise call. A customer enters.

> Sophia, glancing sidelong, saw the assistant parleying with the customer; and then the assistant came softly behind the counter and approached the corner.
>
> "Miss Constance, can you spare a minute?" the assistant whispered discreetly.
>
> Constance extinguished her smile for Mr Scales, and, turning away, lighted an entirely different and inferior smile for the customer.

This observation of Constance's substituted smile does its work in sustaining the life of an episode.

The *Old Wives' Tale* runs to over six hundred pages, covering many happenings and a long span of time, but it is beautifully proportioned and contrived. The kernel of its plot is the fortunes of two sisters, Constance and Sophia Baines. The first of the four books into which the novel is divided is called 'Mrs Baines' and it describes her eclipse and the break-up of the old family organisation of bedridden father, of masterful mother (who runs the shop and disciplines her children), and of placid elder and high-spirited younger daughters. Both daughters defeat their mother in the end: Constance by her obstinate resolution to marry a little beneath her, Sophia by her violent revolt in eloping with the socially superior commercial traveller from Manchester. With the death of her own husband and with Constance's husband in charge of the shop, Mrs Baines has become superfluous in St Luke's Square, Bursley, and goes to live with her sister in the country. The next book, 'Constance', deals with Constance's married life in provincial Bursley, its routine and its excitements, up to her husband's death. The third book, 'Sophia', deals with Sophia's life in France first with her husband and then alone after he has deserted her. It refers to the previous book through both unlikeness and likeness. Paris is different from Bursley, but Sophia, in spite of her revolt, is so much her parents' daughter that she remains a Baines in the alien setting. In the last book, 'What Life is', Constance gets news of Sophia, and the sisters proceed to keep house together: the two main strands of the novel are interwoven. Both are true Baineses, but they have their disputes. Sophia, the thrustful one, wants Constance to give up the dark, inconvenient house in St Luke's Square. But as, in the first book, Constance's obstinacy beneath her placid good nature defeated her mother's wishes about a husband, so now it defeats Sophia's wishes about a home. Constance, the very essence of the provinces, outlives her brilliant sister and gets her death through going out, a sick woman, to vote against a sensible measure of municipal reform. The basic plan is simple and coherent and is seen, through the mass of accompanying details, with exactly the right amount of clarity. It also gets its weight in the right places. The great danger was that the meeting of the sisters, long separated, should fall flat after the narrative of, superficially, the most exciting part of the plot, Sophia's life in Paris during the siege. Bennett triumphs over the danger by making the feelings of the two sisters when they first get in touch through letters stronger and more poignant than any so far revealed. He also shows consummate skill in omitting, measuring with perfect accuracy the jump he can take from one part of the story to another: a skill essential to reducing to manageable proportions the great bulk of his material. For instance, he jumps straight from Samuel Povey's ultimatum to the effect that he will leave Bursley if he is forbidden to court Constance to Mrs Baines's departure, in defeat, to Axe to join her sister after Samuel and Constance have married.

Where Bennett occasionally uses the wrong technique is in over-explicitness. I noted how in the Clayhanger Trilogy he kept harping with too open obviousness on the themes of the effect of time, the degradation of disease, and the wonder of the quotidian. He does not do this in the *Old Wives' Tale*, but he can on occasions err in being too explicit. For instance, when Sophia, now certain that her husband is unreliable and unscrupulous and that he will abandon her some day, steals £200 in notes which she knows he will not miss, thus securing her future independence, Bennett tells us that her conduct was heroic. And when, in the last pages, Constance, sick and racked by sciatica, goes out to vote against municipal federation, he tells us that it was a miracle. In both places he had better have left the reader to make his own comment. But these are small faults in a book that, technically, is a triumph.

(b) *The Theme of Time*

E. M. Forster considers the *Old Wives' Tale* a memorable book and he then says of it:

> Time is the real hero of *The Old Wives' Tale*. . . . Sophia and Constance are the children of Time from the instant we see them romping with their mother's dresses; they are doomed to decay with a completeness that is very rare in literature. . . . Our daily life in time is exactly this business of getting old which clogs the arteries of Sophia and Constance, and the story that is a story and sounded so healthy and stood no nonsense cannot sincerely lead to any conclusion but the grave. It is an unsatisfactory conclusion. Of course we grow old. But a great book must rest on something more than an 'of course', and *The Old Wives' Tale* is strong, sincere, sad, it misses greatness.[1]

As a general statement applying to all literature, Forster's 'of course' is not true, for the triumph of the great artist is to reanimate the commonplace, to exalt the 'of course' to a *gloria*, or in the sober language of Wordsworth to present ordinary things in an unusual aspect. But as a criticism of Arnold Bennett it states an important, though not I believe the main point, about the *Old Wives' Tale*. Time is certainly one of the major themes of the book; and Bennett never lets you forget it. He does indeed feel strongly on the matter and he gives his feelings great prominence. Here is his account of Mrs Baines leaving her home to go to live with her sister at Axe; it has the prominent position of last paragraph of the first book.

---

[1] *Aspects of the Novel* (London 1927), pp. 56-7.

Old houses, in the course of their history, see sad sights, and never forget them! And ever since, in the solemn physiognomy of the triple house of John Baines at the corner of St Luke's Square and King Street, have remained the traces of the sight it saw on the morning of the afternoon when Mr and Mrs Povey returned from their honeymoon—the sight of Mrs Baines getting into the waggonette for Axe; Mrs Baines, encumbered with trunks and parcels, leaving the scene of her struggles and her defeat, whither she had once come as slim as a wand, to return stout and heavy, and heavy-hearted, to her childhood; content to live with her grandiose sister until such time as she should be ready for burial! The grimy and impassive old house perhaps heard her heart saying: "Only yesterday they were little girls, ever so tiny, and now—" The driving-off of a waggonette can be a dreadful thing.

Bennett is evidently very much in earnest, and we respect him for it. But he does not make this culminating paragraph quite convincing. In a writer who excels through strictly prosaic means the fantasy of the house seeing sad sights and retaining their imprint comes oddly, even affectedly, as does the occurrence of the poetical *whither*. Things have gone a little wrong when they most should have gone right. Or take a more elaborate variation on the same theme, the passage that Bennett may well have considered his highest reach in the book, the ruminations of Sophia over the body of her husband, who has died old and in squalid poverty.

What affected her was that he had once been young, and that he had grown old, and was now dead. That was all. Youth and vigour had come to that. Everything came to that. He had ill-treated her; he had abandoned her; he had been a devious rascal; but how trivial were such accusations against him! The whole of her huge and bitter grievance against him fell to pieces and crumbled. . . . By the corner of her eye, reflected in the mirror of a wardrobe near the bed, she glimpsed a tall, forlorn woman, who had once been young and now was old; who had once exulted in abundant strength, and trodden proudly on the neck of circumstance, and now was old. He and she had once loved and burned and quarrelled in the glittering and scornful pride of youth. But time had worn them out. "Yet a little while," she thought, "and I shall be lying on a bed like that! And what shall I have lived for? What is the meaning of it?" The riddle of life itself was killing her, and she seemed to drown in a sea of inexpressible sorrow.

Here again Bennett's sincere and strong feelings are evident, and he moves us up to a point. But only up to a point, for along with our response obtrudes the conviction that the passage is not quite good enough; it cannot quite bear the weight that its author has dared to put upon it. And indeed the weight is huge, for what exacts more than the forthright declaration of large and solemn truths? "Trodden proudly on the neck of circumstance", "drown in a sea of inexpressible sorrow": these are not exactly clichés, but they lack the freshness and the distinction necessary to animate any restatement of the eternal commonplaces. It is not unfair to think in contrast of Shakespeare's

> For beauty, wit,
> High birth, vigour of bone, desert in service,
> Love, friendship, charity, are subjects all
> To envious and calumniating time,

or of Lamb's

> I begin to count the probabilities of my duration, and to grudge at the expenditure of moments and shortest periods, like miser's farthings. In proportion as the years both lessen and shorten, I set more count upon their periods, and would fain lay my ineffectual finger upon the spoke of the great wheel.

Here is less pretence and more distinction, and when we go back to Bennett's aspiring passage we cannot say that Forster's chilly 'of course' is inappropriate.

(c) *Provincial Nonconformity, not Time, the Theme*

If the theme of time really controls the *Old Wives' Tale*, if you attach all the novel's virtue to it, you do right to accept Forster's estimate. But the theme of time is not the main theme. It is as wrong to consider it so as to detach (as so far I have done) Sophia's ruminations on time from Constance's ruminations on life. Both occur in a most prominent place, just before each sister dies: and they are clearly meant to be taken together. This is how Bennett describes Constance's thoughts:

> Constance never pitied herself. She did not consider that Fate had treated her very badly. She was not very discontented with herself. The invincible commonsense of a sound nature prevented her, in her best moments, from feebly dissolving in self-pity. She had lived in honesty and kindliness for a fair number of years, and she had tasted triumphant hours. She was justly respected, she had a position, she had dignity, she was well-off. She possessed, after all, a certain amount of quiet self-conceit. There existed nobody to whom she would 'knuckle down', or could be asked to 'knuckle down'. True, she was old! So were thousands of other people in Bursley. She was in pain. So there were thousands of other people. With whom would she be willing to exchange lots? She had many dissatisfactions. But she rose superior to them. When she surveyed her life, and life in general, she would think, with a sort of tart but not sour cheerfulness: "*Well, that is what life is!*" Despite her habit of complaining about domestic trifles, she was, in the essence of her character, 'a great body for making the best of things'. Thus she did not unduly bewail her excursion to the Town Hall to vote, which the sequel had proved to be ludicrously supererogatory. "How was I to know?" she said.

Here the style makes no high pretences. Bennett intends to suit it to the character he describes, as he intended his heightened style to suit the more passionate and romantic character of Sophia. The superiority of the later passage, the passage about Constance, indicates where Bennett's strength lies. It lies in his power to bring alive and impress on our minds a kindly, commonplace, cheerful, courageous, obstinate, and unadventurous woman. And this woman is part of the means by which he interprets the 'accepted unconscious metaphysic' of the provincial Nonconformity in which he grew up. In fact, the greatness of the *Old Wives' Tale* is that it is the epic expression of what was most central to the English Philistinism that made Matthew Arnold so angry, Midland Nonconformity. It is true that Bennett abandoned both his Wesleyan allegiance and his Staffordshire birthplace and that he was very critical of the things he had given up. But he had lived in the Potteries till he was twenty-one and he could speak for them in a way in which Arnold could not begin to do. Having been bred in Midland Nonconformity he knew it from within; having emerged from it he could view it from without. He was thus fully qualified to be its artistic interpreter.

(d) 'Goodness'

Superficially, it was not a very exciting phase of the Puritan movement that remained for Bennett to interpret. The pioneering phase was over. Nonconformity was no longer persecuted and it no longer held the mercantile initiative. Defoe had celebrated the pioneering phase; Boulton, Watt, and Wedgwood were some of the heroes of its prime. Now, mercantile Nonconformity was powerful, solid, and quiescent, standing more for honest work and sober living than for speculative daring. The initiative was passing to the multiple firms; and there was nothing Nonconformist about them. Bennett marked the beginning of the change by the extinction of the Baines shop, bought up by the Midland Clothiers Company (partly controlled, one surmises, by Bradford Jews); and through his humorous account of the company's methods he celebrated the virtues of what it had replaced.

> The Midland Clothiers Company had no sense of the proprieties of trade. Their sole idea was to sell goods. Having possessed themselves of one of the finest sites in a town which, after all was said and done, comprised nearly forty thousand inhabitants, they set about to make the best of that site. They threw the two shops into one, and they caused to be constructed a sign compared to which the spacious old 'Baines' sign was a postcard. They covered the entire frontage with posters of a theatrical description— coloured posters! They occupied the front page of the *Signal*, and from that pulpit they announced that winter was approaching, and that they meant to sell ten thousand overcoats at their new shop in Bursley at the price of twelve and sixpence each. The tailoring of the world was loudly and coarsely defied to equal the value of those overcoats. . . . Constance was divided between pain and scornful wrath. For her, what the Midland had done was to desecrate a shrine. She hated those flags, and those flaring, staring posters on the honest old brick walls, and the enormous gilded sign, and the windows all filled with a monotonous repetition of the same article, and the bustling assistants. . . .

Twelve-and-sixpenny overcoats! It was monstrous, and equally monstrous was the gullibility of the people. How could an overcoat at twelve and sixpence be 'good'. She remembered the overcoats made and sold in the shop in the time of her father and her husband, overcoats of which the inconvenience was that they would not wear out!

You can say that these passages are about time; it is time that has destroyed the ancestral shop of the Baineses. But much more it celebrates honest work and the sober living that accompanied it, things proper to Victorian England but, within it, to commercial Nonconformity above all. And the key-word is 'goodness', referring primarily to the honesty and durability of the things made but rich in ethical and religious overtones. And 'goodness', not time, is the master-theme of the whole book.

Set against the flouting by the Midland Clothiers Company of the proprieties of trade was the seemliness of the relations between the great Manchester wholesale house of Birkinshaw and the Baines shop in the days of John Baines.

> The relations between the travellers of the great firms and their solid, sure clients in small towns were in those days often cordially intimate. The traveller came with the lustre of a historic reputation around him; there was no need to fawn for orders; and the client's immense and immaculate respectability made him the equal of no matter what ambassador. It was a case of mutual esteem, and of that confidence-generating phenomenon, 'an old account'. The tone in which a commercial traveller of middle age would utter the phrase 'an old account' revealed in a flash all that was romantic, prim, and stately in mid-Victorian commerce.

Here the enkindling word is 'ambassador', perfect in expressing the self-satisfaction of the provinces, the blinkered belief in their own sufficiency. Only, Bennett sees first the virtues of which this self-satisfaction is the defect. It was Matthew Arnold who grew enraged through seeing things the other way round.

And if the clients who had these good relations with their wholesalers were solid and sure, they owned furniture that matched their character. This is how the rooms adjoining the

Baines shop were furnished in the days of the Poveys' prosperity. There was the old drawing-room,

> newly and massively arranged with the finest Victorian furniture from dead Aunt Harriet's house at Axe; two 'Canterburys', a large book case, a splendid scintillant table solid beyond lifting, intricately tortured chairs and armchairs. The original furniture of the drawing-room was now down in the parlour, making it grand. All the house breathed opulence; it was gorged with quiet, restrained expensiveness; the least considerable objects, in the most modest corners, were what Mrs Baines would have termed 'good'.

And the theme is resumed when Sophia clandestinely inspects the parts of Madame Foucault's flat in Paris beyond the room where she had lain ill. The furniture had superficially a grand air, there was an effect of spaciousness, and there was symmetry in the disposition of the pieces.

> But Sophia, with the sharp gaze of a woman brought up in the traditions of a modesty so proud that it scorns ostentation, quickly tested and condemned the details of this chamber that imitated every luxury. Nothing in it, she found, was 'good'. And in St Luke's Square 'goodness' meant honest workmanship, permanence, the absence of pretence. All the stuffs were cheap and showy and shabby; all the furniture was cracked, warped, or broken. The clock showed five minutes past twelve at five o'clock.

(e) *Sophia and Provincial England*

But it is through the way he manipulates an old tale that Bennett most forcefully promotes the themes of 'goodness' and the provincial virtues. The story of the two sisters, one adventurous the other domesticated, is indeed an old wives' tale of perennial recurrence in literature from Antigone and Ismene to Effie and Jeanie Deans, and Bennett's success in making his story hold and delight us as a story helps greatly with the other things he is doing. But the main point of the histories of the two girls is not that they contrast the enthralling life of the Continent with the drab routine of the provinces; it is not even the much more important demonstration (akin to that made by Wordsworth in the *Brothers*) that to the discerning eye life in provincial Bursley is in its way as exciting and as passionately lived as in metropolitan Paris. No, the main point is that the choric theme of English provincialism, set forth directly through Constance at home, is reinforced by Sophia abroad. In fact, the elopement, the execution at Auxerre, and the siege of Paris exist less for themselves than as happenings into which the ethos of Bursley can be interpolated and by contrast heightened. Sophia, far from escaping from Bursley as she intended to do, carries with her a great parcel of it and through this possession achieves her peculiar narrow triumph. It was a brilliant use to which to put the old story, and in it lies the book's undoubted greatness.

But to make Sophia's feat of exportation convincing I must illustrate it. There is a hint of it in the scene in London where she insists on marriage with Gerald before going abroad. This was not what he had intended and he is mildly surprised and annoyed: "he did not reflect that this fragile slip of the Baines stock, unconsciously drawing upon the accumulated strength of generations of honest living, had put a defeat upon him". There you have the epic touch. Sophia in her elopement is not merely a proud woman bound to suffer, but the unconscious heir of multitudes, of which heritage the novelist is the conscious vehicle. As soon as they get to Paris, Sophia is horrified at Gerald's extravagance in buying her clothes.

> The prices frightened her. The simplest trifle here cost sixteen pounds; and her mother's historic 'silk', whose elaborateness had cost twelve pounds, was supposed to have approached the inexpressible! Gerald said that she was not to think about prices. She was, however, forced by some instinct to think about prices —she who at home had scorned the narrowness of life in the Square. In the Square she was understood to be quite without commonsense, hopelessly imprudent; yet here, a spring of sagacity seemed to be welling up in her all the time, a continual antidote against the general madness in which she found herself. With extraordinary rapidity she had formed a habit of preaching moderation to Gerald. She hated to 'see money thrown away', and her notion of the boundary line between throwing money away and judiciously spending it was still the notion of the Square.

Here again there is the epic touch in Sophia's being swayed by communal motives stronger than her individual will. And

Sophia, during the siege of Paris when she runs her boarding-house, by uniting a sense of fairness with frugality and an unerring sense of business, is entirely true to English puritanism. Moreover, she is happy now because she has won her independence and can use her talents, proving herself doubly true to the same spirit. Indeed, in her energy she recalls something of the pioneering phase of English middle-class commercialism. And though she was flighty in her youthful elopement with Gerald Scales she was at bottom puritanical in her passions and could not be satisfied by the sentimental and facile love of Chirac.

> All the time she knew that she wanted love. Only, she conceived a different kind of love: placid, regular, somewhat stern, somewhat above the plane of whims, moods, caresses, and all mere fleshly contacts. . . . She hated a display of sentiment. And even in the most intimate abandonments she would have made reserves, and would have expected reserves, trusting to a lover's power of divination, and to her own! The foundation of her character was a haughty moral independence, and this quality was what she most admired in others. Chirac's inability to draw from his own pride strength to sustain himself against the blow of her refusal gradually killed in her the sexual desire which he had aroused.

This account may individualise Sophia and tell us more about her as a separate character, but all the time it makes her true to the type of morality, in its higher and more refined form, endemic in provincial Bursley.

Most persuasive of all Sophia's home cogitations from abroad is that near the end of her exile when she receives Constance's letter, her first contact with home after many years. This constitutes one of what I think the two culminating places in the *Old Wives' Tale*. It includes not only the ethos of the passage just quoted but the intense and canalised family sense of English puritan provincialism:

> The very spirit of simple love seemed to emanate from the paper on which Constance had written. And this spirit woke suddenly and completely Sophia's love for Constance. . . . Constance's letter was a great letter, a perfect letter, perfect in its artlessness; the natural expression of the Baines character at its best. Not an

awkward reference in the whole of it! No clumsy expression of surprise at anything she, Sophia, had done, or failed to do! No mention of Gerald! Just a sublime acceptance of the situation as it was, and the assurance of undiminished love. . . . Constance had simply written out of her heart. And that was what made the letter so splendid. Sophia was convinced that no one but a Baines could have written such a letter. She felt that she must rise to the height of that letter, that she too must show her Baines blood.

(f) *Constance the Heroine*

One of the great strokes of Bennett's art is not to allow the more taking and more adventurous sister to be the book's heroine; and the second culminating place in the book is where Constance, having yielded to Sophia in taking a holiday in a Buxton hotel, obstinately refuses to continue the holiday by going abroad, with a view to settling ultimately in a cleaner district than the Potteries, and forces a return to the old inconvenient home in St Luke's Square. The episode is not only true to the natures of the two women but it strengthens incalculably the provincial theme. Sophia had indeed carried Bursley into France, but Constance, who was born and died in the same house and who met her death in voting against the federation of Bursley with the rest of the Five Towns, represents provincial tenacity and reaction in its fullest strength. It is fitting, it is essential, that she should both prevail over Sophia's more imperious nature and that her flabbier, slower body should outlast the enduring slimness and grace of Sophia's. Thus surviving, Constance is a most powerful symbol of the habits of thought that Bennett knew from within and, even in escaping from, continued to admire.[1] Through her he best created the heroic impression.

(g) *Religion*

Finally, there is religion. Bennett was well aware of the vices of Midland Nonconformity: its pretences, its tyranny, its lethargy. He had nothing to learn from Mark Rutherford. And on a superficial reading one might conclude that those vices

---

[1] Constance was heroine of the novel as originally planned. See Pound, *op. cit.*, p. 181.

were all that he could see or cared to mention. But a closer reading reveals a subtle and pervading sense of the sway of religion over the minds of his people. The more thoughtful folk of Bursley felt about religion as Sophia felt about love. If it was to be any use, its real sway must be taken for granted, guessed at, not discussed. Thus in the nature of things there cannot be much overt reference in the book to genuine religious feeling. But consider the connotations of this minute detail in a passage already quoted: the detail of the Midland Clothiers using the *Signal* as their pulpit. The use of the word *pulpit* suggests first blasphemy by the new firm and second a religious foundation for the honest mercantile methods of the private firms the Midland Clothiers were in process of superseding. Those methods may have been practised largely from habit and thoughtless imitation: yet they were partly grounded on the awesome religious principles of not burying your talent and of giving an account of your acts on the Last Day. The fact of that grounding might be forgotten, but it was part of at least the unconscious metaphysic of the chapel-goers of Bursley: and Bennett makes us subtly aware of it.

Not that overt references to religion are lacking. When his cousin, Daniel Povey, murdered his drunken wife, Samuel Povey in the stress and excitement of the event turned his thoughts to religion.

"Ah!" he reflected in the turmoil of his soul: "God is not mocked!" That was his basic idea: God is not mocked! Daniel was a good fellow, honourable, brilliant; a figure in the world. But what of his licentious tongue? What of his frequenting of bars? (How had he come to miss that train from Liverpool? How?) For many years he, Samuel, had seen in Daniel a living refutation of the authenticity of the old Hebrew menaces. But he had been wrong, after all! God is not mocked! And Samuel was aware of a revulsion in himself towards that strict codified godliness from which, in thought, he had perhaps been slipping away.

Samuel said nothing, but his thoughts typified the hidden thoughts of a multitude.

And Constance ultimately held similar opinions about Sophia. For all the generosity of her letter and of her assumption that in their common widowhood they should live together she considered Sophia as one who had sinned. Standing over Sophia's dead body she feels an overwhelming pity, but a pity involving a judgment.

> Sophia's charm and Sophia's beauty—what profit had they been to their owner? She saw pictures of Sophia's career, distorted and grotesque images formed in her untravelled mind from Sophia's own rare and compressed recitals. What a career! A brief passion, and then nearly thirty years in a boarding-house! And Sophia had never had a child; had never known either the joy or the pain of maternity. She had never even had a true home till, in all her sterile splendour, she came to Bursley. . . . Hers had not been a life at all. And the reason? It is strange how fate persists in justifying the harsh generalizations of Puritan morals, of the morals in which Constance had been brought up by her stern parents! Sophia had sinned. It was therefore inevitable that she should suffer. An adventure such as she had in wicked and capricious pride undertaken with Gerald Scales, could not conclude otherwise than as it had concluded. It could have brought nothing but evil. There was no getting away from these verities, thought Constance.

Matthew Arnold's lament at the overplus of Hebraism as against Hellenism in the England of the Philistines may serve to corroborate the sober truth of Bennett's presentation.

(h) *Epic Quality*

That, then, is the virtue of the *Old Wives' Tale*, its successful rendering of a choric feeling, the feeling of provincial puritanism. Bennett reinforces that rendering by many vivid pictures of communal feeling and activity: the excitement over the escaped elephant, the loiterers outside the murderer's house. In fact, he supports his special choric theme by convincing you that life of all kinds was being transacted in the Five Towns. He gives us the entry into a community. He also validates his choric theme by bringing to life the people who act it. One of his triumphs is the crabbed and bitter Mr Critchlow, who' is kept alive throughout the book: another is his succession of domestic servants; even in the days of their abundance Bennett grasped as few did the sway they exerted over the happiness of their employers as well as the pathos of their position. In spite of the sobriety of his style Bennett showed great warmth of human sympathy.

Of tragedy he was not a master; and that lack of mastery indicates pretty well his limitation. His type of realism could never capture the accents of passion that Defoe's could attain; he could never invent so sublime a touch as Defoe's "two shoes that were not fellows" among the drowned sailors' effects washed up on the island. When he attempts the tragic he opens himself to Forster's comment, 'of course'. Thus the *Old Wives' Tale* cannot rank among the very greatest novels; it is the least exalted of the novels I have dwelt on in this book. But within its limits it is, past doubt, an authentic epic.

8

Joyce: 'Ulysses'

(i) *Potential Epic Qualities*

I AM not likely to have anything new to say on *Ulysses*; and too much has been written on it in recent years: I would gladly leave it alone. However, as a work demanding consideration as an epic it simply cannot be evaded. Joyce gave seven years to it after less ambitious ventures and put into it his main resources. It is massive; and in certain ways its parts are knit together with surpassing complexity. And when Joyce later called his *Ulysses* "an epical forged cheque on the public for his own private profit" he was talking ironically and meant that he had epic ambitions and that his effort brought him little acknowledgment from the wider reading public.

Not that I need take Joyce's claims too seriously, for it is most unlikely that his notion of an epic was identical with the one I work on. But at least it seems as if he thought that in his way he was doing what the classic writers of epic had done before him, if only through the sheer massiveness of his artefact and the concentrated and sustained pains he spent on it. Nor is *Ulysses* the freakish and isolated portent it was once considered. It is as richly ancestored as any other would-be epic, though the ancestry may be uncommonly miscellaneous. Melchiori[1] is right in thinking that it goes behind the main conventions of nineteenth-century prose fiction to the more fluid and experimental conditions of the eighteenth century, when prose fiction included things as unlike the fiction of the nineteenth century as *Gulliver's Travels* and *Tristram Shandy*, while Smollett in *Humphry Clinker* anticipated,[2] through the distortions of Winifred Jenkins's epistolary language, many of Joyce's linguistic habits. Joyce is also the child of the nineteenth century,

---

[1] Giorgio Melchiori, *The Tightrope Walkers* (London 1956), pp. 34-52 (the essay on *Joyce and the Tradition of the Novel*).
[2] Others besides Melchiori have noticed this anticipation.

but through its poetical or poeticising sides. If he broke violently with the current tradition of prose fiction, if he was utterly at odds with the realism of Bennett and Wells and Galsworthy, he compensated by developing, in his prose, methods that had existed, at least embryonically, in the poetry or poetical prose of the last hundred years or more. If Pater gave him the hint of how to manipulate fiction with extreme sophistication and fastidiousness the poets had displayed the art of passing abruptly from one style to another. As well as *Idylls of the King*, Tennyson wrote *Maud* with its astonishing stylistic fluctuations. With *Faust* in the background and *Peer Gynt* much closer, there is nothing surprising in a technique that mixes realism and high or wild fantasy. However different, *Ulysses* and the *Dynasts* are parallel products. Or for the rudiments of a general 'stream of consciousness' technique imagine *Tithonus* succeeded by *Caliban upon Setebos*. It is therefore not surprising that Joyce went to work in certain ways, however new or surprising or monstrous or overwhelming the thing was that through those ways he brought into being. As a potential epic writer he is not conspicuously untraditional.

There is a vast variety of matter in *Ulysses*, a lavishness which at once satisfies a part of one epic essential. It might be objected that the variety, however dazzling, leaves all kinds of things untouched. Indeed Joyce has been narrowed into[1] a "great destructive satirist" and *Ulysses* into a book that serves to show up the "moral failures of modern civilization". But there is a good deal besides destruction and a good deal of morality which, though it is often in difficulties, cannot be described as a failure. While Joyce does not mitigate a single shortcoming in Leopold and Marion Bloom, he allows them positive qualities and is devoid of satire in so doing. Stephen did not fail in morality when he refused to kneel and pray for his mother's soul as she lay dying. On the contrary, he acted only too strictly in accordance with it and through that very strictness was harassed by remorse. And if Joyce pitilessly mauls a bogus kind of Irish patriotism through embodying it in the violent and ridiculous figure of the Citizen in the Cyclops episode he presents in all sincerity, lucidity, and fear the

[1] See Richard M. Kain, *Fabulous Voyager* (Chicago 1947), pp. 2, 3.

ineluctable dilemma of the genuine Irish patriot through the visions that Stephen has of his own country and of its overshadowing and overbearing neighbour. Granted that epic is possible when dealt with from the side of comedy, satire, and farce, *Ulysses* does not fall short in point of sheer substance.

There is no need to quarrel with the high value that competent readers generally have put on what Joyce has made of parts of that substance. At his best he can heighten the trivial as successfully as Chaucer and Cervantes. True, he often inflates and bores as well as heightens; but the episode of the Citizen's attack on Bloom at the pub, told by an Irish proletarian and punctuated by Joyce's own fantasy, ending with the double theme of Bloom, pursued by the dog, escaping in the cab and Bloom as Elijah rapt into heaven, touches sublimity from the side of the trivial as surely and triumphantly as the *Miller's Tale*. Such an episode does not constitute an epic but stands all ready to contribute to the heroic impression. Even the episodes that bore can do the same. The Eumaeus scene in the cabmen's shelter, written in quintessential ditchwater of the stalest English, becomes hideously boring. But it has the quality of the bore who hypnotises his victim and it ends by overpowering all opposition. There is something heroic, however monstrous, in the completeness with which Joyce, rounding up every straggler from the great army of worn phrases, propels the total array through the cowed and unresisting corridors of the reader's brain. And one could justify other episodes in similar ways. No doubt of the greatness of some of the parts.

(ii) *Is it a Whole?*

It is when the reader scans the whole that doubts begin. Can he honestly believe that this whole is greater than the sum of its parts? Let me consider a few of the supposed agents of unification and try to gauge their effects.

Edmund Wilson's exposition[1] of the Odyssean parallels in *Ulysses* has brought comfort to many beginners in their initial fog and bafflement. Here, they felt, was something at least to

---

[1] *Axel's Castle* (New York 1931), section on James Joyce.

get hold of. Yet I doubt whether these parallels brought them comfort in any strictly literary way. Their function was to reassure, to assert that there was some unperceived order in the great heap, in fact to give the reader's mind a rest, to allow his slower digestive processes to work and to encourage him to try again after recuperation. As to the parallels themselves, the better you know the book, the less you find them to matter; the more academic and the less fundamental they show themselves. There may be a likeness between the curiosity of Bloom and the curiosity of Odysseus, but it does not mean more than, for instance, that between the pedantic epicurean-ising of the Rev. Dr Opimian in *Gryll Grange* and of the Rev. Dr Middleton in the *Egoist*. This undoubted derivation of Dr Middleton does little to explain the *Egoist* and nothing to hold it together. Marion Bloom and Stephen Daedalus can be nominally approximated to Penelope and Telemachus through some of the situations in which they find themselves, but in their natures they are violently opposed to their counterparts. Nor can you argue that there is point in this violent opposition, that here opposition is resemblance turned inside out, for not all resemblance is excluded. For instance, Telemachus and Daedalus are alike in being adolescents feeling their way towards mature strength. The detailed parallels with the *Odyssey* may have helped Joyce with his massive task; they may have led to the things that really matter. But the reader notices them only with an effort, and an effort that merely distracts him from fundamental comprehension. And, if this is so with the comparatively plain references to the *Odyssey*, how much more with the correspondences of the various episodes to the parts of the human body. Such a piece of revived medievalism may have helped to satisfy the appeten-cies provoked in Joyce by his Jesuitical training and to keep him to his task, but its help to the reader is negligible. And the same principle applies to the other complexities that have been and will be detected.

Then there is the notion that the changed relations between Leopold and Marion Bloom at the end, and the hint that Stephen may find himself at home in their house and make something different of it, have a wide-spreading and pervading effect. There are many possible ways of defining these changed relations. You can say that Bloom's Odyssean experiences through his long day have purged and strengthened him. At the beginning, in ignoble subservience to Marion, he brought up her breakfast to the bed in which he was shortly to be made once more a cuckold, but during the day he survived various trials, laid the troublesome ghost of his dead infant son through his new friendship with Stephen, and ended by demanding that next time Marion shall bring him *his* breakfast in bed. He has asserted himself and shown that he will put his house in order. Or you can follow Edmund Wilson in the crowning importance he gives to Marion, to her promiscuity and the things into which it is destined to issue. However low she has stooped, he says

> she will tend to breed from the highest type of life she knows: she turns to Bloom, and, beyond him, toward Stephen. This gross body, the body of humanity, upon which the whole structure of 'Ulysses' rests—still throbbing with so strong a rhythm amid obscenity, commonness and squalor—is laboring to throw up some knowledge and beauty by which it may transcend itself.[1]

My trouble with these expositions is that they do not arise naturally from the whole text of the book but have to be arrived at by isolating and exaggerating a few passages. From the whole text we have not the least assurance that Stephen would do other than bore Marion Bloom stiff or that Leopold will oust Blazes Boylan. Joyce's reference (a few sentences before she begins her soliloquy) to Marion as reclining in the attitude of Gea-Tellus does indeed prove that he meant her to be a symbol as well as a woman, but there is a split between what she has signified to the reader through the great course of the narrative and the symbolic significance with which Joyce now invests her. Marion as Gea-Tellus has no pervasive unifying power whatever. If our thoughts of her, before the very end of her soliloquy, are tempted to stray anywhere outside the bounds of the book, it is not to the Demeter figure of the mythologies but to the *Canterbury Tales* and especially the Wife of Bath.

[1] *Ib.*, p. 224.

A reason why we should be cautious in accepting so clear and confident a symbolic theory as that of Edmund Wilson is that it is distressingly easy to manufacture others. For instance, why should the theme not be: Stephen-Joyce renounces Ireland, with its ineffectiveness and its oppressive subservience to Rome and England, for cosmopolitanism (Bloom), towards which the world is progressing, and Nature and neo-paganism (Mrs Bloom)? You could make a good case for this theme by selective reference; and yet it suffers from the common defect of having no living correspondence with the genuine findings of the intelligent, unprejudiced, unacademic reader.

Then there is the notion that Joyce makes *Ulysses* a whole by indicating the progress of day and night through the different episodes. It is true enough that he does in places make us greatly aware of time of day: of morning over the sea, of evening as Gerty MacDowell and the rest of the party leave the beach for the city. But it is also true that not all of the episodes are specially appropriate to the hour of their transaction, that throughout much of the bulk of many episodes we do not think of the time of day at all, and that the temporal shift is not capable by its unaided self of binding together so vast and heterogeneous a matter. The great bulk of the two episodes after the Circe episode in Night-Town, that of Eumaeus in the cabmen's shelter and of Ithaca in the Blooms' house, corresponds singularly ill to the exhaustion appropriate to the small hours and to the reaction from the wild vitality of the brothel. However flat or heavily judicial the tone, it is maintained with a vitality that may serve the general purposes of the novel but which can only damage any supposed unity achieved by the progress of the hours. Then what has Stephen's discourse on Hamlet, for instance, to do with the time of day? Little enough in the mind of the ordinary reader. And as for the general competence of a mere time-sequence to give unity, think of Blake's *Echoing Green*, where the time-sequence, obviously very important indeed, is yet subservient to and only completed by the greater motive of satisfaction, of fulfilment in tiredness.[1] Can it be said that the changing hours in *Ulysses* are supported by a greater, pervasive theme? I doubt it.

[1] See my *Poetry Direct and Oblique* (London 1945), pp. 12-15.

Walter Allen, at the beginning of his section on *Ulysses*[1] in the *Living Novel*, admits that even after repeated readings he cannot see it as a whole: he has not yet decided whether "it is a whole or a magnificent ruin". And he represents a good many readers. But later he seems to go back on his uncertainties and to find the unifying agent in Joyce's Dublin. Dublin pervades the characters, making us through them ever aware of it: "*Ulysses* is an intensely local novel." It is the world of Dublin on a June day in 1904 "that gives *Ulysses* its real unity, over and above the fictitious one of the bases in Homer, for it links organically through the shared experiences of the scene character with character". That is true up to a point, though Joyce's Dublin makes a far less clear impact than Hardy's Casterbridge or Conrad's Sulaco, being rather a continuous background, or something pervasive like a miscellany of smells. But such continuity of background establishes no more fundamental unity than does the progress of the hours. In no profound sense is *Ulysses* 'about' Dublin, which is presented in too chaotic a guise to mean anything in particular, even chaos itself.

Indeed, if *Ulysses* is ever to represent itself to readers as an accomplished whole, it will be from a side very different from any of those just mentioned, a side not concerned with subject-matter and parallels of episodes but with matters of form and pervasive, ruling sensations, with matters closer to music than to the representational arts. If such a side *can* be developed it will account, for instance, for the greatly increased length of the episodes that form the second half. It always remains possible that *Ulysses* is organised through a governing rightness difficult to divine and perceptible only after prolonged acquaintance, through a tact in making this episode follow that and lead up to the other that satisfies some very profound instinct for order, the kind of tact that I guess unconsciously guided Spenser when he ordered the *Fairie Queene* as he did[2] and which may have told him that he had better stop at the end of six books. The comparison with Spenser, whose motives are so utterly hidden from us and whose acts had he lived are

---

[1] pp. 337-42.
[2] See my *English Epic*, pp. 286-7.

so utterly unpredictable, may serve, if it does no more, to indicate the highly conjectural nature of this paragraph.

(iii) *Its Affinities*

Actually I think those right who hold that the quest for unity is vain and that we should approximate Joyce not to the authors of single great works whose significance lies largely in the union of abundant matter and rigorous shaping but to the great fantasts and exuberants, to Rabelais, Sterne, and the Goethe of the second part of *Faust*. I could even add *Hamlet*, the influence of which on *Ulysses* is a commonplace. There are various things in *Hamlet* to give it a shape, but you have only to put it alongside *Othello* to see that the shaping contains a relatively small proportion of the total meaning. In fact, the two plays illustrate a simple and basic difference between two kinds of art. I have described the difference elsewhere,[1] as it touches Shakespearean tragedy:

> The artists by the richness of their presentation enlarge the range of experience comprehensible by the unaided efforts of the ordinary person, and by the form of their presentation suggest some order in this range of experience. A great artist will excel in both functions. But, however great he is, he has to compromise and to adjust the scope of one function to that of the other. . . . To apply the above to Shakespeare's tragedies. *King Lear* is the play where the balance is most evenly struck. In *Othello* the content of experience is less and the emphasis falls more on the ordering. *Hamlet* is best understood as a play less of ordering than of sheer explication or presentation, as a play presenting the utmost variety of human experience in the largest possible cosmic setting.

I do not intend to make a close comparison with *Hamlet*, but I think that the relation of *Hamlet* to *Othello* provides a helpful analogy with the relation of *Ulysses* to *Nostromo* or *Paradise Lost*. It is the richness of presentation that first matters in *Ulysses*, and that richness includes much that has very properly been called poetry. Bloom's exaltation when warmed by the Burgundy, the phallic account of the rise of the rocket as he

[1] *Shakespeare's Problem Plays* (London 1950), p. 28.

watches Gerty at evening by the seashore, the last pages of Marion Bloom's soliloquy are conspicuous examples of Joyce's poetry. *Ulysses*, in fact, is a great farrago of superb epiphanies (as he called them) such as these, and of comedy, satire, farce, pedantry, and crushing boredom; something not to apprehend whole but a store, or a quarry, to which to return again and again with the certainty of finding something fresh. The first comment I heard on *Ulysses*, years ago, soon after it came out, was from the eminent classical archaeologist (who could have been among the first of living critics if he had cared to put his mind to literature instead of Greek vases) J. D. Beazley. He is given to the laconic in his aesthetic comments; and his verdict on *Ulysses* was: "There's a lot of detail." I do not think this verdict has been superseded.

If *Ulysses* appeals chorically it is not to the author's own compatriots. It has established no grip on the minds of Irishmen at large. On the other hand it is a genuinely cosmopolitan book and has commanded through the world much wonder and some affection, even if its vogue has been confined to the austerer intellectuals or to those who pretend, whether successfully or not, to be such. Since *Ulysses* suffers from an unusual amount of fashion-bred, hypocritical adulation, it is not easy to detect the true cause of its appeal. Part of it consists in the technical innovations. However well ancestored *Ulysses* may be, it went back violently and explosively on the prevailing technique of the novel. It gave the revolutionary thrill. Secondly, if it failed to speak for a nation, it had a great deal to say about what have been vulgarly called the disinherited mind and the displaced person. Stephen Daedalus fits the first phrase pretty well, and Leopold Bloom the second. Stephen hopes to gain an inheritance through art and Bloom achieves a precarious attachment to an alien society, but the strength of their appeal consists less in any positive qualities they may own than in being misfits. It could be maintained that *Ulysses* speaks for all those who today feel themselves exiles from the society in which they are set.

The last remark confronts us with the question whether such negative feelings as the sense of exile or of failure to fit in can be the substance of the epic. I think not. As, according to

Nietzsche, tragedy cannot exist in an age of doubt, so epic must embody some positive faith. Through lacking such a faith *Ulysses* cannot be epic. For the same reason it has no need for a clear, unifying pattern. Form and substance both point to the same conclusion.

Ian Watt on the Novel Form

WATT's position is briefly this: the early eighteenth-century novel in England contains so many new features and constitutes so violent a break with any past literature that it must amount to a new literary kind. Some of these features are: the rejection of traditional plots, the individualising of the persons (typified in substituting actual for conventionally classical or descriptive names, e.g. Moll Flanders for Philoclea or Castiza), a new sense of time and of space (consider the *Faerie Queene* as an example of a narrative quite devoid of that sense), the impression of actual experience, and an 'authenticity of report' in the language used to describe events or states of mind.

I reject Watt's position for two reasons, the second much more important than the first.

(1) I find the break less violent than Watt does. I doubt, for instance, if the novel has in actual fact rejected traditional plots. Any borrowing has been less open and less conscious; but there has been much repetition of essential themes. Again, if the *Faerie Queene* lacks the sense of time and place, Chaucer's *Troilus and Criseyde* displays it, not to speak of many of the *Canterbury Tales*. And what of Shakespeare and a character like Mrs Quickly? Even if her name expresses what was expected of her as a hostess, can it be said that her words show any sign of lacking a sense of time and place?

> Thou didst swear to me upon a parcel-gilt goblet, sitting in my Dolphin-chamber, at the round table, by a sea-coal fire, upon Wednesday in Wheeson week, when the prince broke thy head for liking his father to a singing-man of Windsor, thou didst swear to me then, as I was washing thy wound, to marry me and make me my lady thy wife.

I admit that the impression of actual experience is rarer before than after the eighteenth century, but the strength of an impression does not depend entirely on frequency of occurrence. Through a few memorable passages Langland takes us

197

into the very heart of actual experience: and these passages are never swamped by the mass of didactic allegory that surrounds them; they retain all their force when we contemplate the total effect of his poem. As for authenticity of report, there is plenty of it in Elizabethan drama.

(2) When Watt sets forth the things that make the novel into a new literary kind I find he sets forth instead the innovations common to the whole trend of things in the early Augustan age. And he appears in one place at least to admit this. It is where (p. 24) he notices that the increased time-sense shown in the novel is duplicated in history. In spite of this parallel, Watt holds that time-sense is a differentia of the novel. The truth is that the time-sense certainly existed earlier, that it was greatly developed at the period in question, and that in its developed form it has appeared all over the place. If it is powerful in history, it is powerful in the *Prelude* and in Arnold Bennett's *Milestones*. It is also powerful in Bennett's *Old Wives' Tale*; but why it should here be a differentia as being found in a novel and not in *Milestones* as being found in a play I cannot see. The same principle holds good for the impression of actual experience. It is a commonplace, for instance, that, with the eighteenth century, nature need no longer serve only as a moral emblem or a setting sympathetic to human passion but can give the impression of authenticity, and it is the habit to point to Lady Winchelsea.

Finally, there is no guarantee that the attributes of the English novel of the early eighteenth century are destined to endure. They are certainly not all present in the novels of Goldsmith, Jane Austen, Emily Brontë, Meredith, and Stevenson. The symbolic novels of Kafka and Rex Warner are radically different; and who dare say that their kind may not prevail at some future date?

In disagreeing with Watt on the nature of the novel I am not expressing an adverse opinion on his book as a whole. Its virtues are found in its erudition and in its contribution to literary sociology, and these are outside the scope of my remarks.

Conrad's Costaguana

THOSE who admire *Nostromo* sufficiently to read it several times carefully are apt to grow interested in the details of the geography. It is hardly a critical interest like that in the book's geographical intensity; for instance the question whether the promontory of Azuera bounded the Golfo Placido on the north or on the south is not critical like the question whether the promontory itself captures our imagination. However, though indubitably marginal, interest in the geography of Costaguana can be a spontaneous growth which a critic is justified in serving provided he does not make it out to be other than it is. I have had the curiosity to plot out some of the geography of Costaguana, and I give my findings for the benefit of anyone similarly interested; but I do so in an appendix to make it clear that those findings are not 'criticism'.

Conrad wrote to Cunningham Graham[1] that "Costaguana is meant for a S. American state in general; thence the mixture of customs and expressions". He might have mentioned the geographical mixture too, for the country is composed of a medley of details drawn from all sorts of places in Central and South America. What is certain is that it lies between San Francisco to the north and Valparaiso to the south, while it borders on both oceans. It contains a mountain topping the snow-line of a hot latitude and in its remote parts it is the source of great rivers. Its name suggests Costa Rica and Central America; but the absence of great rivers kills the suggestion. South of Panama, the Republic of Columbia touches both seas but has the wrong shape. Other names suggest Central America. There is an Azuero peninsula in Panama; there is a town called Sulaco in Honduras; there are Rincons in Panama, Mexico, and in the American state of New Mexico; and there is a Golfo Dulce in Costa Rica. Costaguana,

[1] See G. Jean-Aubry, *Joseph Conrad, Life and Letters* (London 1927), i, p. 338.

then, is an imaginary republic on one or other side of the Isthmus of Panama but so imagined as to be unidentifiable.

Sulaco, where the action takes place, is the capital of a province of that name and it faces the Pacific Ocean. It lies near the northern frontier of Costaguana, beyond which is a 'sister republic'. It is bounded by some kind of hills to the north and on the west by the Cordillera topped by the snow-peak of Higuerota. There is also a coastal (and presumably much lower) range of mountains. The two ranges coalesce north of Sulaco, but stand wide apart to the south, leaving between them the Campo. Eighty miles eastward over the Cordillera is Sta. Marta, the capital of the Republic. The direct road there is over the Cordillera up the Ivie Valley and over the Entrada Pass, close to the peak of Higuerota; it is a dangerous way because of the precipices and of the blizzards. Sta. Marta is in a fertile valley and is within easy reach of a port on. the Atlantic Ocean. Round Sta. Marta and to the south the main population of Costaguana lives. There is an easier but much longer way from Sulaco to Sta. Marta than the direct one over the Entrada Pass. This is by way of Cayta, the principal port of Costaguana, situated five hundred miles south of Sulaco on the Pacific. Eastward of Cayta the Cordillera either ceases or is no longer at all formidable as a barrier. Anyhow, there is easy land communication from Cayta to Sta. Marta. A long way south of Sta. Marta and perhaps south-east of Cayta is the Province of Entre-Montes with its capital, Nicoya, the native province of the Monteros. Esmeralda is a small port between Sulaco and Cayta but much nearer Sulaco, important as head of the main cable from San Francisco to the western provinces. There is a branch cable to Sulaco.

The approach to Sulaco from the Pacific is through the Golfo Placido, a semicircular bay in a coast-line running roughly north and south. The rocky peninsula of Azuera bounds the bay on the north, and the cape of Punta Mala bounds it on the south. The national frontier runs a little way north of Azuera. At the head of the gulf there is an opening that leads into the oval of Sulaco harbour; and outside the opening are the three rocky islands, the Isabels. The smallest of these, Hermosa, a bare rock, lies between the Great Isabel and the harbour. The greatest breadth of the oval is north to south. At the harbour entrance to the north is an old fort, and near the north shore is the village of Zapiga. On the flat, south shore there are palm trees. Ships approaching Sulaco from north or south do not see the town till they reach the harbour-mouth. Sulaco lies opposite the entrance and is backed by the Cordillera. At the time of the story's main action the harbour equipment consisted of a jetty built out into the shallow water by the O.S.N. Steamship Company. Near it on the land was the Customs House. A little way inland was the pallisaded yard of the new railway. There was an ancient track connecting port and town and entering the town by one of the gates in the old fortifications. Midway, on the track and near the new railway, was the house of Giorgio Viola.

Within the walls of Sulaco, Constitution Street runs from the harbour gate, into the Plaza. In it is the Casa Gould with the Casa Corbellán opposite. The Plaza is flanked on one side by the Cathedral and contains on the opposite side the offices of the *Porvenir* newspaper, Anzani's shop, and the Amarilla Club. Opposite the end of Constitution Street is the Alameda with its trees, containing the statue of Charles IV and leading to the gate for the mountains or the campo. The road that issues from it is the old royal road leading first of all to the village of Rincon, five or six miles away.

There were two branches of the railway from Sulaco, perhaps dividing at Rincon. One was to go over the Entrada Pass to Sta. Marta, the other south, presumably to Cayta. Nostromo travelled by an engine on the second branch for over a hundred miles to rail-head on his way to Barrios at Cayta. Past Rincon the road to the San Tomé mine, three or four miles distant, diverged from the royal road. The mine was part way up the lower slopes of the Cordillera. The approach to it lay across a ravine; and the bridge marked the entry to the mine's private domain. Near the bridge but beyond and above it were the villages and workshops attached to the mine. Zigzag paths led to the mine-entrances higher up in the face of the mountain.

South of Rincon and between the Cordillera and the campo was the forest area of Los Hatos, where Hernandez and his band were at large. Farther away still and not definitely to be located is the "wild and waterless" Bolson de Tonoro, his ultimate fastness and his refuge before venturing so near to Sulaco as Los Hatos.

When Decoud travelled with his newly bought rifles from Europe, he went entirely by sea. This was a roundabout way and much farther than the usual route through the Atlantic port and Sta. Marta. He went through the Straits of Magellan by a main line steamer and then changed somewhere on the west coast into a local steamer going north and calling ultimately at Sulaco.

This account has been compiled from many statements and hints throughout the book. It is partly conjectural and is very open to correction. A conjectural plan of the district of Sulaco appears opposite.

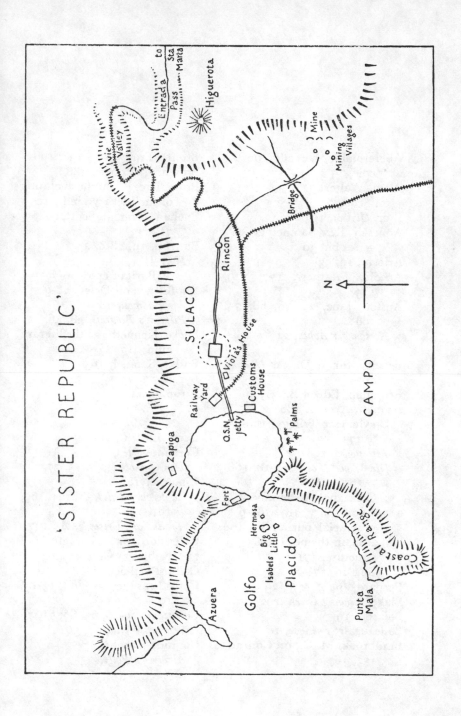

Index